GREAT COOKING— GREAT CONVENIENCE, TOO

with an Amana Radarange® Microwave Oven

The microwave oven is the most exciting new major appliance for the home today. It saves time and energy, saves on electricity, and has amazing versatility for all kinds of cooking.

This cookbook shares with you a wealth of creative new recipes for the microwave oven, using the full potential of this "miracle worker" appliance.

All recipes were tested in an Amana Radarange oven. To use these recipes in a microwave oven with a different cooking power, an easy time conversion table is included.

And if you do not yet cook with microwaves, conventional cooking directions have been provided, too.

Enjoy!

THE *Amana* GUIDE TO
GREAT COOKING
WITH A
MICROWAVE OVEN

POPULAR LIBRARY • NEW YORK

TABLE OF CONTENTS

TABLE OF CONTENTS

Part I

ABOUT THE MICROWAVE OVEN

CHAPTER 1:

Introduction to Microwave Cooking

Every year hundreds of thousands of homemakers are adding the fastest, most modern device to their kitchens—the microwave oven. They like its convenience, its speed of operation, its energy-saving economy, and its compact beauty.

While microwave ovens are considered an essential part of nearly two million American kitchens in 1975, it was not always so.

How it all started

The first microwave oven was produced in Raytheon Company laboratories in 1945.

The discovery of the principle of microwave cooking resulted from wartime research in radar. During World War II (and ever since) Raytheon was one of the leading producers of radar equipment. In 1945 the late Dr. Percy L. Spencer of Raytheon, while testing a radar vacuum tube, realized that the microwave energy it generated produced heat. He thought it might cook food. He sent out for a chocolate bar, it was said, and put it in front of the radar tube. The chocolate immediately melted.

So Raytheon developed and patented a microwave oven which it trademarked "Radarange," designed for use in hospitals and other mass-feeding situations. These first microwave ovens were large and expensive to build.

Amana Refrigeration, Inc., became a subsidiary of Raytheon in 1965. Working with Raytheon engineers, Amana introduced the world's first 115-volt countertop domestic model in 1967, the Amana Radarange Microwave Oven.*

Since then consumer interest in microwave cooking has soared. Happy owners have found that their microwave ovens far exceed their original expectations and provide them with a wide range of delicious foods. They have found that this new appliance is the ultimate method for reheating leftovers to "just-cooked" goodness; for quick-fixing snacks and single-portion meals; for thawing and cooking—from hard-frozen to the table—in just minutes, and for preparing complete, nutritious family dinners—fast.

How microwave ovens perform the miracle of "heatless" cooking

Cooking with microwaves differs from conventional cooking in that it does not utilize the *direct application of heat* to cook food.

---

*"Radarange" is the registered trademark of Amana Refrigeration, Inc., for all of its microwave oven products.

In a conventional oven, or on a surface burner, the food cooks by the transfer of heat from the burner, or from the heated oven air, or—in boiling—from the water to the food. Heat reaches the center of the food slowly from the outside to the inside. When the center is the required temperature, the food is cooked.

In a microwave oven, microwave energy is absorbed by the food. This energy agitates the molecules to produce heat *within the food itself,* cooking it throughout very rapidly.

Microwaves are reflected from metal but pass through substances like glass, china, paper, or non-metallic plastics.

In food, the microwaves cause the food molecules to heat, and thus—literally—to cook themselves.

Microwaves penetrate the food from all directions. As they reach the surface they generate heat. The energy not absorbed by the surface layers passes to the next layer, and this process continues through to the center with the microwave power becoming less intensive in each successive layer of molecules. Food prepared in the Radarange oven is not cooked from the inside out but is cooked *throughout at the same time* with more cooking on the exterior of the food. Therefore, it is possible to prepare a roast that is brown on the exterior and rare, medium, or well done in the center.

Why cook with microwaves

Microwave cooking is not just an improvement in conventional cooking methods. It is an entirely new cooking concept, a new process of introducing heat to foods. Amana calls it "the greatest cooking discovery since fire."

Save time. Radarange oven cooking literally takes hours out of kitchen chores. Most foods—even complete meals—are cooked in one-fourth the time it normally takes in a conventional range!

The Amana Radarange oven will cook a 22-pound (continued page 11)

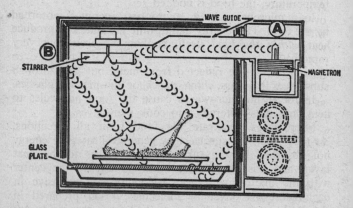

Food is cooked in the Amana Radarange® Microwave Oven by the absorption of microwave energy.

"Microwave" is a term applied to electro-magnetic waves within a specific frequency band. They are similar to radio, television, and infrared waves.

In the Amana Radarange® oven, microwave energy is generated from electrical energy in a vacuum tube operated as an oscillator, called a "magnetron," and directed into the oven cavity. The energy reflects off the walls and bottom of the oven cavity. The

In this drawing, energy emitted by the magnetron antenna (A) strikes the stirrer, a slowly revolving metal fan (B), which reflects the power, bouncing off the walls, ceiling, back, and bottom of the oven, distributing it evenly throughout the cooking cavity. Power enters the food from all sides to cook it evenly. The microwaves pass through glass, paper, or plastic without effect, but are reflected from metal and absorbed in food.

Thanksgiving turkey to perfection in just 7 minutes per pound compared to 35 minutes per pound for conventional electric or gas ovens. A medium-rare 7½-pound beef roast takes only 41 minutes. Heated rolls, 10 seconds. Lobster tail goes from frozen to serving in 5½ minutes. And melted butter for it in 10 seconds. The Radarange oven cooks a 2½ pound chicken in 16 minutes and, to go with it, 5 ears of corn-on-the-cob in 8 minutes (no boiling water needed).

But there is more time-saving with a Radarange oven than fast cooking.

No after meal clean-up of metal pots and pans! As long as you cook with microwaves, you will never have to scour another pot or pan. These are never used.

Cook and serve on dinnerware. You can prepare food in almost any material or container that is not metal or that does not have metal trim or hardware. You can use glassware, dinnerware, paper plates, paper napkins or plastic containers. The microwaves pass right through these materials to concentrate all the energy on the food. The cooking utensil will be "servingly" warm from the food on it.

Easy oven clean-up. The sides, top, and bottom of the Radarange oven cooking cavity do not get hot. That means that splatters or spills will not burn themselves to the sides of the oven. You need only wipe with a damp cloth to clean.

Save energy

Because the microwaves heat only the food, not the oven and the air around the food, your kitchen stays far cooler than during conventional cooking. This saves on the work your air conditioner has to do, and on your electric bill.

Cooking in a Radarange oven is fast and efficient. Energy is consumed only while food is actually cooking— and cooking is fast!

A conventional range, whether gas or electric, is a

major consumer of energy. The basic reason is that the conventional cooking process itself is inefficient. On the surface unit the element is heated, it heats the bottom of the pan (some heat is lost into the air), which then heats the food. In the case of boiled items, the water is heated, then thrown away. A conventional oven is preheated to heat the air, which heats the outside of the food, and, eventually, heats the inside of the food to the temperature required to cook it. Heat is lost and power wasted every time the oven door is opened.

Compared to cooking in a Radarange oven, the conventional way is slow and inefficient. The microwave oven, of course, does not heat the air. There is no preheating of an empty oven, and the utensil is not heated first. Instead, the microwave energy is absorbed by the food and converted directly into heat.

Extensive tests by major electric utilities and the Amana Test Kitchen show energy savings from 50 percent to 75 percent for the Amana Radarange oven, compared to conventional electric ranges.

Here are some tested examples of electricity savings made in cooking with the Radarange oven compared to conventional electric ranges:*

Energy savings will vary with the portion and type of foods. The foods shown are typical foods and portions. Some other foods or portions will fall below 50 percent savings; others will be considerably more than 75 percent savings.

---

*Comparison tests were made by leading West Coast and Midwest utilities and the Amana Ann MacGregor Test Kitchen using the appropriate conventional cooking techniques in an electric oven, range top, or electric fry pan.

Compare Energy Savings:

Meat and Poultry

58% Savings—Beef Goulash
61% Savings—Chicken, Shake and Bake
70% Savings—Hamburger Patties —4 (4 oz. ea.)
79% Savings—Meat Loaf
63% Savings—Roast (4 lb.), Sirloin Tip
54% Savings—Steak, Pepper in pouch
51% Savings—Turkey (11 lb.)
62% Savings—Turkey Broccoli Bake

Vegetables

76% Savings—Broccoli (10 oz.), boil in bag
78% Savings—Corn, Frozen in Pouch
64% Savings—Potato, Baked— 4 (2 lb. 1 oz.)
68% Savings—Potatoes, Scalloped
77% Savings—Squash, Acorn (2 lbs.)

Fish/Seafood

90% Savings—Fish Fillets, French
63% Savings—Fillet of Sole
71% Savings—Lobster Tails, Frozen—4
88% Savings—Shrimp Chow Mein Dinner, Frozen
81% Savings—Tuna, Casserole

Desserts

75% Savings—Baked Apples—4
91% Savings—Brownies, Mix in a Pan
85% Savings—Cake, Almond Chocolate Cake Mix
76% Savings—Cake, Coffee
61% Savings—Cake, Two Layer, Yellow

If an average family of four were to use the microwave oven exclusive of any other cooking means, the electric power consumed in a year would be approximately 300 kilowatt hours. In contrast, the Electrical Energy Association lists typical annual consumption of a conventional electric range at 1175 kilowatt hours. The Radarange oven annual savings then, amount to 875 kilowatt hours— or a savings of 74.5 percent.

The Radarange oven can quickly pay for itself in electrical savings alone. There is no installation cost. *Regular 115-volt household current is all the Radarange oven requires.* It just plugs in: no costly special wiring.

Taste, nutrition enhanced

Since foods cook much faster, while cooking inside and out at the same time in the Radarange oven, they *dry out less.* Several university studies have commented on the

13

superior retention of vitamins with microwave cooking. One reason is the avoidance of the use of large quantities of water in cooking vegetables, potatoes, and fruits. Many nutrients are dissolved in cooking water and lost in conventional cooking. Microwave cooking avoids this problem by requiring little or no water. In addition, the lower surface temperature of the foods and the shorter cooking times reduce the evaporation and breakdown of many food nutrients.

The same factors that promote the retention of nutrients act to preserve delicate color and flavor compounds. Vegetables and fruits retain brighter colors and fresher flavors.

From frozen to ready-to-eat in minutes. Food freezers, either as part of a refrigerator-freezer combination or as separate appliances, are commonplace nowadays. Frozen foods are part of our everyday life. Now for the first time you can take hard-frozen food from the freezer and thaw it in the Radarange oven, cook it in the Radarange oven, and serve it in a matter of minutes.

CHAPTER 2:

Good Management of Your Microwave Oven

There are certain practices that you can—and should—
follow. Some of the tips in this chapter will make cooking
easier. Others will help you select the best utensils and
provide proper care for your oven. Still others are tables
that will serve as shorthand references to guide you in
everyday cooking. All will help you to truly great cooking
with a Radarange microwave oven.

Proper utensils

You may use in the Radarange oven most of the wide
variety of utensils made of non-metallic material, and
utensils that do not have metal trim or hardware. USE
THESE:
- —Heat-proof glassware.
- —Dinnerware (without metal trim).
- —Ceramic ware such as Corning Ware®.

15

—Corelle Living Ware®—*except closed-handle cups*.
—Paper products: paper plates or towels, and napkins to cover foods that might splatter or absorb grease.
—Plastic containers (hot foods may distort shape of some types—oily or greasy foods may remove glaze from some types).
—Cooking bags and pouch packs. (Use *string tie*, not the small metal tie that is packed with cooking bags. *Pierce a hole* in the bag for steam to escape or it may expand and burst.)
—Plastic wrap may be used to cover food being reheated or for other *short-time* use. If it remains too long in the oven, some types of plastic wrap may become sticky or shrink. *Pierce a hole* in the wrap. *Do not use a wrap with foil edges.*

Do Not Use:

—Metal pots or pans.
—Ceramic dishes with metal trim or handles.
—Foil pans.
—Aluminum foil.
—Corning Ware Centura® dinnerware.
—Corelle Living Ware® closed-handle cups.
—Melamine dishes.

If you use metal, you may damage the utensil as well as the microwave oven's magnetron tube.

Metal reflects microwaves. It will keep portions of the food from cooking. Those areas would not cook enough while other areas would be overcooked.

In addition, metal will reflect microwave energy back from the oven's cooking cavity to the magnetron tube, causing it to overheat and have a shortened operating life. This tube is the most costly part of the microwave oven. If it is properly cared for, it will provide many years of perfect service.

Also, if you operate the Radarange oven empty, the tube may overheat: without a food load to absorb the energy, it reflects back to the magnetron and causes possible damage.

Hints to Make Cooking Even Easier

There are several things you can do as general practice that will make cooking in the Radarange oven easier.

Microwaves are attracted to the moisture in food, and they take the path of least resistance. Therefore, there is more concentration of microwaves in some areas due to the composition of the food itself. For a more even distribution of microwaves in the food, and thus more even cooking, some change of position of the dish, or the food itself, should be standard practice. Rotating a dish, turning a roast, stirring a casserole—all achieve the desired result.

Single small load. When heating a single small item, such as a strip of bacon or a potato, all the microwave penetration is concentrated on that item. Cooking time is short, and manipulation is usually unnecessary.

Wrapping. When heating a hot dog in the bun, freshening pastries, or thawing yeast items, it has been found that wrapping the item in a napkin distributes the generated heat more evenly throughout.

Covering. Some foods, such as vegetables, will cook more evenly in the microwave oven if the container is covered. Glass, plastic, or paper may be used to cover cooking containers. Paper towels on bacon and other foods will reduce spattering. These recipes state when to cover; unless so indicated, covering is not essential during cooking.

Dish size. The use of a larger container than may seem necessary is specified in many of the recipes using dairy or milk products. This prevents boiling over and spillage.

Dish Rotation. Rotation of the cooking dish is usually a 90° or 180° turn to allow more even cooking.

Stirring. Most casseroles, sauces, etc., should be stirred while cooking to distribute the heat.

Factors that affect microwave cooking time

The recipes in this book give you a guide to cooking times in the microwave oven. Factors that have influence on cooking time include:

Type of Food. Foods vary in the amount of heat required to raise their temperatures. For example, the energy required to raise the temperature of tomatoes a given number of degrees is about twice that required by an equal weight of ground beef. Therefore, almost twice as much time would be required to cook tomatoes as ground beef.

Volume of Food. As the volume of food is increased, the time required to cook or heat the food increases proportionally. If twice the amount of food is placed in the range, it will take almost twice as long to cook.

Starting Temperature of Food. This is an important factor in microwave cooking. Cold or refrigerated foods require longer cooking than foods at room temperature.

Size and Shape of Food. When the shape of food is irregular, the thin narrow parts heat faster than thicker parts. Food with protruding pieces (turkey, etc.) may require shielding strips of foil over wings and legs to prevent overcooking or drying out.

Density of Food. Light, porous items, such as bread and pastries, will absorb energy faster than more compact items of the same weight, thus needing only seconds to thaw or heat.

Arrangement of Food. As far as possible, foods should be placed in the oven on the same level—and well separated. Do not stack. When heating foods cooked in layers (peas, small vegetables, etc.) use a large dish, and spread the food out to reduce the number of layers.

Conversion of conventional recipes for microwave oven cooking

Conventional cooking consists of applying heat to cook the food. You dial a temperature, allow time for the cooking device to reach that temperature, and then you place your prepared food into it. Time, temperature, and heat are taken into consideration in allowing for the cooking period. Microwave cookery allows you to do away with temperature and heat.

Most food is prepared in the same manner that you would for conventional cooking. We suggest when converting your favorite recipe, that you start with approximately ¼ the conventional cooking time. For instance, one piece of bacon, 1 minute. A 7½ ounce baking potato, approximately 4 minutes. To bring 1 cup of water to a boil, approximately 1¼ minutes; 2 cups, about 2½ minutes. (This serves as a good standard for judging the cooking time of most liquids.) Allow less cooking time, and test the food. One note of caution: always undercook rather than overcook. A carry-over cooking process, because the food retains heat, will continue after the food is out of the oven. Overcooking causes food to become dry and dehydrated.

Browning

Roasts, hams and turkeys will brown nicely and look the way you want because they are cooked in the Radarange oven for relatively long periods.

There are a few foods that are not in the Radarange oven long enough to brown, and may need color additives. Paprika may be used on poultry. Steak sauce, Worcestershire sauce, soy sauce or liquid browning and seasoning sauce like Kitchen Bouquet and Gravy Master may be used on meats and other dishes (for instance, casseroles and stews) when you want added color. Coating mixes such as Shake 'n Bake® may also be used. Toppings of toasted bread crumbs or cracker crumbs add color and crispness to casseroles.

Vanilla brushed on a pie shell before baking will add color.

The Browning Skillet

The Amana Browning Skillets are footed microwave dishes, with covers, made expressly for use in the Radarange oven, by Corning®. There is a 9½-inch skillet and a round 6½-inch skillet that has a handle. Both have a special coating on the outside bottom. The coating interacts with the microwave energy and becomes hot. When used as directed, the temperature is self-limiting and is less than 600° (about the maximum of an electric fry pan). The cover is Pyrex® brand heat-resistant clear glass.

When preheated in the Radarange oven, the skillet can be used for browning meats, fowl, fish, sandwiches, pancakes, and frying eggs, to name just a few. The skillets also make excellent casseroles and are good for cooking vegetables and other foods. They are "freezer-safe" and can go directly from the freezer to the Radarange oven without waiting to thaw.

You may order these and other Radarange oven accessories from your Amana retailer.

Heating of Convenience Foods

The following table of suggested heating times for prepared foods, both frozen and refrigerated (in some cases, for room temperature foods), is intended to serve as a guide for use in heating foods in a Radarange oven. Exact heating times will vary with the amount of food being heated, the temperature of food at start of the heating time and the type of container or dish being used. Watch foods carefully while they are being heated and check them often for proper serving conditions. Remove foods while they appear to be still slightly underdone or underheated.

Note: All cooking times given are for Amana Radarange oven models with 675-watt cooking power. To convert for microwave ovens with different cooking power, please consult the table on page 29.

FOOD	MEASURE AND/OR WEIGHT	HEATING TIME	SPECIAL INSTRUCTIONS
Roast Beef Hash			
Frozen	2 servings (11½ oz.)	6¼–6¾ minutes	Heat uncovered. Stir after 4 minutes.
Refrigerated	"	2¼–2¾ minutes	Heat uncovered. Stir after 1½ minutes.
Individual Meat Pies (Completely baked)			
Frozen	1 serving (8 oz.) in 10-oz. glass casserole	6½–7 minutes	Heat uncovered. Turn dish once or twice.
Refrigerated	"	2½–2¾ minutes	"
Stuffed Peppers with Tomato Sauce			
Frozen	2 servings (14 oz.)	6½–6¾ minutes	Heat uncovered. Turn dish once or twice. Let stand 5 minutes before serving.
Refrigerated	"	2½–3 minutes	Heat uncovered. Turn dish once or twice. Let stand about 3 minutes before serving.
Chow Mein			
Frozen	2 servings (14 oz.)	7–7½ minutes	Cover. Stir after 5 minutes. Let stand 4–5 minutes before serving.
Refrigerated	"	2½–3 minutes	Cover. Stir after 1½ minutes. Let stand a few minutes before serving.
Escalloped Chicken & Noodles			
Frozen	2 servings (12 oz.)	6–6½ minutes	Heat uncovered. Stir after 5 minutes. Add topping after stirring.
Refrigerated	"	2–2½ minutes	Heat uncovered. Stir after 1½ minutes. Add topping after stirring.
French Fried Potatoes			
Frozen	3 servings (9 oz.)	4½–5 minutes	Spread potatoes one layer deep on paper toweling laid on paper plate. Turn several times during time in Radarange oven.
Refrigerated	"	2¼–2½ minutes	"

FOOD	MEASURE AND/OR WEIGHT	HEATING TIME	SPECIAL INSTRUCTIONS
Baked Stuffed Potatoes			
Frozen, cooked	1 medium (6 oz.)	3¼–3¾ minutes	Heat uncovered. Turn several times.
	2 medium (12 oz.)	7–7½ minutes	"
Refrigerated	1 medium (6 oz.)	1–1½ minutes	Heat uncovered. Turn at least once.
	2 medium (12 oz.)	2–2½ minutes	"
Green Peas in Cream Sauce			
Frozen, uncooked	3 servings	6–6½ minutes	For commercial frozen, add liquid as directed on package. Cover to cook. Stir after 5 minutes. Let stand, covered, for a few minutes before serving.
Refrigerated, cooked	"	1½–2 minutes	Cover. Stir after 1 minute. Let stand, covered, for a few minutes before serving.
Green Peas and Celery			
Frozen, uncooked	3 servings	4½–5 minutes	Add 1 tbsp. water. Cover. Stir after 2 minutes.
Refrigerated, cooked	"	2–2½ minutes	If no liquid, add 1 tbsp. water. Cover. Stir after 1 minute.
Glazed Carrots			
Frozen, uncooked	3 servings	5½–6 minutes	For commercial frozen, add liquid as directed on package. Heat, uncovered. Stir gently after 4 minutes.
Refrigerated, cooked	"	2–2½ minutes	Heat, uncovered. Stir gently after 1 minute.
Creamed Onions			
Frozen, uncooked	3 servings	5½–6 minutes	For commercial frozen, add liquid as directed on package. Heat, covered. Stir after 4 minutes.
Refrigerated, cooked	"	2–2½ minutes	Heat, covered. Stir after 1½ minutes.

FOOD	MEASURE AND/OR WEIGHT	HEATING TIME	SPECIAL INSTRUCTIONS
Hamburger and Frankfurter Buns			
Frozen	1 bun	24–26 seconds	Heat, uncovered, on a paper napkin or serving dish.
	2 buns	45–47 seconds	"
	4 buns	1¼–1½ minutes	"
Room temperature	1 bun	10–12 seconds	"
	2 buns	18–20 seconds	"
	4 buns	34–36 seconds	"
Chicken & Onions in Gravy			
Frozen	1 serving (¼ of a 3-lb. broiler-fryer with gravy)	8–10 minutes	Cover. Turn dish several times. Let stand 5 minutes before serving.
Refrigerated	"	2½–3½ minutes	Cover. Turn dish several times. Let stand 3 minutes before serving.
Hamburger Patties, Cooked			
Frozen	1 4-oz. patty	1¼–1½ minutes	Heat uncovered. Be careful not to overcook.
	2 4-oz. patties	2¼–2½ minutes	"
Refrigerated	1 4-oz. patty	45–50 seconds	"
	2 4-oz. patties	1¼–1½ minutes	"
Individual Dinners (with meat and 2 vegetables)			
Frozen	Not recommended		
Refrigerated	1 average serving	3–5 minutes	Heat, uncovered, on serving plate. Watch carefully as heating time will vary with foods.
Individual Dinner of Mexican foods, with tamales, beans, chili gravy, and rice			
Frozen	1 average serving	6–6½ minutes	Heat on serving dish, uncovered. Turn frequently.
Refrigerated	"	2¼–2¾ minutes	"

FOOD	MEASURE AND/OR WEIGHT	HEATING TIME	SPECIAL INSTRUCTIONS
Macaroni and Cheese			
Frozen	1 large serving (16 oz.)	4½–5 minutes	Heat uncovered. Turn dish or stir several times.
Refrigerated	"	1½–2 minutes	Turn dish or stir at least once.
Sliced Cooked Roast Beef, Turkey, and similar meats			
Frozen	4 oz.	1–1¼ minutes	Let stand a couple of minutes before using. Meat will not be completely thawed, but sufficiently to separate slices and serve cold. If desired to serve hot, increase time in Radarange oven.
	8 oz.	2–2¼ minutes	"
Refrigerated	4 oz.	1½–1¾ minutes	Sufficient time to heat meat enough for serving hot. If gravy or sauce is included, increase time in Radarange oven.
	8 oz.	2¾–3¼ minutes	"
Corn Soufflé or Pudding (unbaked)			
Frozen	2 servings (12 oz.)	11–12 minutes	Heat uncovered. Turn frequently during time in Radarange oven.
Refrigerated	Not recommended		
Waffles, baked			
Frozen	1 waffle, 2½" x 3½"	18–20 seconds	Heat, uncovered, on a paper napkin or serving dish.
	2 waffles, 2½" x 3½"	35–40 seconds	"
Room temperature	1 waffle, 2½" x 3½"	10–12 seconds	"
	2 waffles, 2½" x 3½"	18–20 seconds	"
Dinner Rolls, baked			
Frozen	2 medium	20–25 seconds	Heat, uncovered, on a paper napkin or serving dish.
	4 medium	40–50 seconds	"
	6 medium	60–70 seconds	"
Room temperature	2 medium	10–12 seconds	"
	4 medium	18–20 seconds	"
	6 medium	24–26 seconds	"

FOOD	MEASURE AND/OR WEIGHT	HEATING TIME	SPECIAL INSTRUCTIONS
Doughnuts, plain			
Frozen	2 medium	40–45 seconds	Heat, uncovered, on a paper napkin or serving dish.
	6 medium	1¾–2 minutes	"
Room temperature	2 medium	14–16 seconds	"
	6 medium	40–45 seconds	"
Cinnamon Snails, baked			
Frozen	1 large	45–60 seconds	Heat, uncovered, on paper napkin or serving plate.
	2 large	1½–2 minutes	"
Room temperature	1 large	15–25 seconds	"
	2 large	30–45 seconds	"
Danish Pastry, baked			
Frozen	4 servings (8 oz.)	1¾–2 minutes	Heat, uncovered, on paper napkin or serving plate.
Room temperature	"	45–60 seconds	"
Apple Dumplings, baked			
Frozen	2 medium servings	5–5½ minutes	Heat in serving dishes. Let stand 5 minutes before serving.
Room temperature	"	1½–2 minutes	Heat in serving dishes. Let stand a minute or so before serving.
Fruit pie, baked			
Refrigerated	8-inch size	5½–6½ minutes	Let stand 5 minutes before serving. (This time is sufficient to serve pie warm; if higher temperature is desired, increase time in Radarange oven.)
Refrigerated	"	2½–3 minutes	Let stand a couple of minutes before serving. (This time is sufficient to serve pie warm; if higher temperature is desired, increase time in Radarange oven.)

Gourmet cooking techniques

Several Radarange oven models offer the versatility of "slow" gourmet cooking through use of "Automatic Defrost" or "Slo Cook" controls. These enable you to:
—do slow cooking.
—create full-bodied sauces and soups.
—tenderize less expensive cuts of meat.
—thaw and serve convenience foods effortlessly.
—preserve the original goodness of leftovers.
When you use these controls, the Radarange oven turns itself "on" for a given number of seconds, then "off" for a given number of seconds alternately. The results are similar to those achieved by long simmering on a range top (as with soups, sauces, puddings, etc.) or by slow roasting. With the Radarange oven, however, you will accomplish these time-consuming cooking methods in far less time and without constant attention.

Gourmet slow-cooking techniques are fully explained in the instructions and owner's manual provided with these Radarange oven models.

Thawing frozen foods

Microwave ovens do a superior job of thawing frozen food—and do it remarkably fast.

Many foods such as cakes, breads, frozen vegetables, cookies, and other small-volume items should be taken quickly from the frozen to cooked state with the microwave oven. No more manipulation is required than for cooking fresh foods—just slightly more time.

Other larger bulk items require alternating heating and "resting" periods while heat is equalized through the food. This helps prevent the food from being cooked on the surface or edges while the inside is still being thawed.

Specific instructions for Radarange oven thawing of frozen fruits, vegetables, meat, fish and seafood, and poultry are found in the introductory pages of the appropriate chapters of this book. As a general rule, carefully follow defrosting instructions provided in the owner's manual for your microwave oven. And remember—always transfer frozen foods from foil or meal containers to suitable microwave oven utensils before placing in the oven.

Automatic defrost control

Automatic defrost is a new convenience feature on several Amana Radarange microwave oven models. It makes defrosting frozen foods easier by eliminating the need for manually turning the oven "off" and "on" to accomplish alternating heating and "resting" periods. The control cycles the Radarange oven "on/off" automatically. Detailed automatic defrost cycle instructions are provided with these Radarange oven models.

Reheating "planned overs"

With the Radarange oven, leftovers become "planned overs." You can quickly return a refrigerated or frozen serving to the same peak flavor it had originally. You will want to consider this advantage when you plan and prepare your meals. In a sense, you become the manufacturer of your own line of convenience foods. (And that can mean savings in your pocket these days.) Here are a few guidelines to help you:

—Use container suitable for Radarange oven when freezing or refrigerating your own dinners or casseroles.

—When reheating, cover the container with plastic film or wax paper. When using plastic film, pierce with a fork before cooking.

—Use the automatic defrost cycle to reheat leftovers. This can eliminate constant watching and stirring, as well as the chance of overcooking the edges.

—Stir the food once at the end of the cooking period if possible. If not, allow for a carry-over cooking period after the cooking time has elapsed.

—To heat baby foods, remove desired amount from jar and place in appropriate Radarange oven cooking utensil. Baby bottles may also be warmed.

Cooking power output/cooking time

The "cooking power output" rating of a microwave oven is the power that is absorbed by the food and converted into heat. You can generally find this rating for your microwave oven stamped on the oven's serial number plate or in your owner's manual.

The higher the power output, the faster the heating. If you double the power output, you double the cooking speed—and cut the cooking time in half.

All recipes and cooking times in this book were developed and tested in an Amana Radarange® microwave oven with a power output rating of 675 watts. If you own a microwave oven with a lower power rating, refer to this table:

EQUIVALENT TIMES CONVERSION TABLE

Manufacturer's Microwave Oven
Power Output Rating:

650–700 Watts (Recipe times in this cookbook)		550–600 Watts (. . . Convert to:)		450–500 Watts (. . . Convert to:)	
Min.	Sec.	Min.	Sec.	Min.	Sec.
	10		11.5		14
	20		23		28
	30		34.5		42
	40		46		56
	50		57.5	1	10
1	00	1	09	1	24
2	00	2	18	2	48
3	00	3	27	4	12
4	00	4	36	5	36
5	00	5	45	7	00
10	00	11	30	14	00
20	00	24	00	28	00

As a rule of thumb, add *20 percent* to the cooking time for a 550–600 watt microwave oven; add *40 percent* for a 450–500 watt model. All cooking times are approximate. Actual best times will depend on your tastes as well as the various other factors already mentioned. Undercook and test as you would normally.

Part II

RECIPES

CHAPTER 1:

Appetizers, Soups, and Chowders

When you have a microwave oven you need never again bore your guests before dinner with a dull assortment of crackers covered with cheese spread! Instead, you can bring in a trayful of hot flavorful canapés and hors d'oeuvres that have been popped in and out of the Radarange oven with incredible speed. (The easy preparation was done hours ago, and you are as fresh and cool as

31

the flowers that decorate your table.) As for your guests, they may be too busy enjoying each delectable morsel to compliment you until after the last one has disappeared and dinner is announced!

Just the names will entice you. Ham and Chutney Fingers, Tipsy Stuffed Eggs, Oysters Casino, Curried Cocktail Scramble, Peking Spareribs—and there are more.

CHICKEN ROLL

¼ pound chicken livers
1½ pounds chicken breasts, boned
½ pound boiled ham
3 eggs, beaten
1 teaspoon dry mustard
¼ teaspoon nutmeg
Pinch allspice
2 teaspoons salt
⅛ teaspoon white pepper
1 tablespoon minced parsley
1 tablespoon minced onion
⅓ cup packaged seasoned crumbs, divided
2 cups chicken broth

Place chicken livers in dish with ½ cup hot water. Cook in Radarange oven uncovered for 1 minute until slightly firm. Drain. Put livers, chicken and ham through fine blade of meat grinder. Thoroughly mix together ground meats with eggs, seasonings, and 4 tablespoons crumbs. Chill mixture, then shape into roll about 10″ long and 3″ thick. Place chicken roll on piece of cheesecloth; sprinkle with remaining crumbs; roll up, tying ends. Arrange roll in 2-quart oblong glass dish. Warm chicken broth in oven 3 minutes; pour over chicken roll. Cook in oven 15 minutes, turn dish 180° after 7½ minutes cooking. Turn roll over, cook 15 minutes more, turn dish around 180° after 7½ minutes cooking. Cool roll and refrigerate overnight. Remove cloth, sprinkle roll with paprika; cut in thin slices to serve. Makes about 6 dozen thin slices.

Conventional Cooking:
1. *Arrange wrapped roll in shallow baking dish, add chicken broth.*
2. *Bake in moderate oven, 350°, covered with aluminum foil, about 75 to 80 minutes. If broth cooks away before roll is cooked, add ½ cup hot water or broth to dish.*

CRABMEAT CANAPÉS

1 can (7½ oz.) crabmeat,
  drained and flaked
1 tablespoon minced green
  onions (scallions)
1¼ cups shredded Swiss
  cheese

½ cup mayonnaise
1 teaspoon lemon juice
¼ teaspoon curry powder
6 dozen crisp round crackers

Thoroughly mix together all ingredients except crackers to make a spread. Place ½ teaspoon crabmeat mixture on each cracker round. Arrange 12 at a time on paper plate or towels. Cook in Radarange oven 30 seconds. Repeat with remaining crackers. Makes 72 canapés.

Conventional Cooking:
1. Prepare as directed. Arrange spread crackers on cookie sheet.
2. Bake in a moderate oven, 350°, 8 to 10 minutes.

CURRIED COCKTAIL SCRAMBLE

1 cup butter or margarine
  (2 sticks)
2 tablespoons Worcester-
  shire sauce
1 teaspoon curry powder
2 teaspoons onion salt
½ pound mixed nuts

½ pound Spanish peanuts
2 cups wheat cereal squares
2 cups rice cereal squares
2 cups Cheerios
1 package (5 oz.) thin pret-
  zel sticks

Mix together butter or margarine and seasonings in glass bowl; heat in Radarange oven 1 minute. Mix remaining ingredients in large bowl or casserole. Drizzle with hot seasoned butter, stirring and tossing until ingredients are coated. Cook uncovered in oven 8 minutes, mixing and tossing at 2-minute intervals. Makes about 3 quarts.

Conventional Cooking:
1. *Melt butter or margarine in skillet over moderate heat. Stir in seasonings. Combine remaining ingredients in large baking dish or roasting pan. Pour seasoned butter over all. Stir and toss to coat ingredients.*
2. *Bake uncovered in a moderate oven, 350°, 20 to 25 minutes, stirring several times.*

HAM AND CHUTNEY FINGERS

2 cups minced cooked ham
⅓ cup chutney, finely
  chopped

¼ cup mayonnaise
2½ dozen 1" x 2" toast
  fingers

Mix together ham, chutney, and mayonnaise. Spread mixture on toast fingers. Arrange 15 on flat plate or paper towels; cook in Radarange oven 1 minute. Repeat with remainder. Makes 30 appetizers.

Conventional Cooking:
1. *Prepare as directed. Arrange fingers on baking sheet.*
2. *Bake at 350° for 7 to 8 minutes.*

HAWAIIAN FRANKS

½ cup soy sauce
1 teaspoon ground ginger
2 teaspoons sugar
1 teaspoon instant minced
  onions

1 can (1 lb.) pineapple
  chunks, drained
¼ cup pineapple juice,
  drained from chunks
1 pound cocktail franks

Mix together first four ingredients to make a marinade. Drain pineapple chunks; reserve ¼ cup liquid. Add to marinade. Combine marinade and franks in shallow glass baking dish. Refrigerate 3 to 4 hours, stirring several times. Add pineapple chunks to franks. Cover dish; cook in Radarange oven 3 minutes. Stir, cook 3 minutes more. Serve hot in sauce with bamboo skewers for spearing. Makes about 5 dozen appetizers.

Conventional Cooking:
1. Turn mixture into fry pan.
2. Cook over moderate heat about 10 minutes, stirring often. Marinade should be slightly reduced and thickened.

HOT SEASHORE DIP

4 jars (5 oz. each) "Old English" cheese spread
2 cans (7 oz. each) minced clams, partially drained
½ cup diced green pepper

½ cup chopped scallions
¼ teaspoon Tabasco sauce
¼ teaspoon garlic powder (or to taste)

Mix together all ingredients in a bowl. Cook 6 minutes, uncovered, stirring twice. Serve hot with crackers for dipping. Makes 4 cups.

Conventional Cooking:
1. Place cheese in top of double boiler over hot water. Cook over low heat until cheese melts, about 15 minutes. Stir in remaining ingredients.
2. Cook an additional 10 minutes or so, stirring often.

KEFTEDES

1½ pounds ground beef
½ cup soft fresh whole wheat bread crumbs
⅓ cup minced onion
2 tablespoons chopped parsley
2 eggs, beaten
¼ teaspoon seasoned pepper
¼ teaspoon cinnamon

¼ teaspoon allspice
1 teaspoon salt (or more to taste)
1 tablespoon water or wine
2 to 3 drops mint extract
¼ teaspoon bottled browning sauce
2 tablespoons water

Mix together all ingredients except browning sauce and water. Cover loosely; refrigerate 3 to 4 hours. Shape mixture into bite-size balls, arrange in oblong baking dish in a single layer. Brush with half of browning sauce mixed with water. Cover with paper towels; cook in Radarange oven 5 minutes. Stir, brush on more browning sauce; cook 3 minutes more. Serve hot with cocktail food picks for spearing. Makes about 5 dozen little meat balls.

Conventional Cooking:
1. Heat 2 tablespoons shortening in large skillet; add meatballs. Cook over medium high heat for a few minutes. Stir and turn meatballs until browned on all sides.
2. Reduce heat to low. Cover skillet; simmer meatballs about 10 to 15 minutes.

LITTLE PIZZAS

6 English muffins
Butter or margarine
⅔ cup catchup
12 slices salami
12 slices round sliced process cheese

2 tablespoons grated Parmesan cheese
2 teaspoons Italian herb seasoning

Split muffins in half evenly; spread with a little butter. Top each half with a spoonful of catchup, salami slice, and 1 slice of cheese. Sprinkle with Parmesan cheese and seasoning. Arrange 6 halves in a 2-quart oblong dish. Cook uncovered in Radarange oven 1¼-minutes, turn dish around and cook another 1 to 1¼ minutes. Repeat with remaining pizzas. Serve hot. Makes 3 to 4 appetizers.

Conventional Cooking:
1. *Prepare as directed. Arrange little pizzas on cookie sheet.*
2. *Bake in hot oven, 400°, about 5 to 6 minutes until cheese melts.*

LIVER AND BACON ROLLS

1 pound chicken livers	*6 slices bacon, cooked and*
2 hard-cooked eggs	*crumbled (page 75)*
1 teaspoon minced onion	*Salt and pepper to taste*
2 tablespoons soft butter or	*Toasted bread crumbs*
margarine	

Cook livers in water to barely cover in the Radarange oven 4 to 5 minutes, stirring twice. Cover with paper towel, since they pop. Livers should be soft and pink inside. Drain. Press livers and eggs through sieve, or put through food mill. Mix well with onion, butter, and crumbled bacon; season to taste. Chill mixture several hours.

Toast several slices of bread; crumble fine. Shape tablespoons of chilled mixture into little cylinders; roll in toast crumbs. Place 12 little rolls on paper plate in oven. Cook uncovered 1 minute 45 seconds to 2 minutes. Turn plate 180° after half of cooking time. Repeat with remaining rolls. Makes 24 appetizers.

Conventional Cooking:
1. *Prepare as directed. Arrange on cookie sheet.*
2. *Bake in a moderate oven, 350°, about 8 minutes.*

MEXICAN DIP

1 can (1 lb. 14 oz.) red kidney beans
2 tablespoons vegetable oil
2 tablespoons finely chopped
onion

1 cup process cheese,
grated
½ teaspoon salt
2 teaspoons chili powder
(or more to taste)

Drain beans, reserve ⅓ cup bean liquid. Pour reserve liquid
into blender jar. Add beans and blender-chop briefly to make
a fairly smooth mixture. Heat oil and onions in 1½ quart
casserole; cook 1½ minutes in Radarange oven. Add beans
to onions; cover, cook in oven 3 minutes. Stir in cheese and
seasonings. Cook 2 minutes. Serve hot with corn chips. Makes
2 cups.

Conventional Cooking:
1. Mash beans with oil and a little bean liquid. Turn into a
   saucepan. Cook and stir over medium heat for 4 to 5
   minutes. Stir in cheese and other ingredients.
2. Reduce heat to low. Stir mixture over low heat until cheese
   is melted and mixture thickened.

NACHOS

1 can (15½ oz.) refried
beans
1 package (5½ oz.) tortilla
chips

4 to 6 ounces cheddar
cheese, grated
Thinly sliced olives or
jalapeno peppers

Spread about 1 teaspoon refried beans on each chip. Top
with 1 teaspoon cheese and a thin slice of olive or jalapeno
pepper. Place eight on paper plate or paper towel, heat in
Radarange oven 30 seconds, or until cheese is melted. Serve
warm. Makes about 4 dozen.

Conventional Cooking:
1. *Arrange prepared tortilla chips on cookie sheet.*
2. *Bake in moderate over, 350°, 4 to 5 minutes until cheese melts.*

OYSTERS CASINO

2 dozen freshly opened oysters*

3 slices bacon, cooked and crumbled (page 75)

2 tablespoons minced onion

2 tablespoons minced green pepper

2 tablespoons minced parsley

2 tablespoons minced celery

1 teaspoon Worcestershire sauce

Dash Tabasco sauce

1 tablespoon butter

¼ cup seasoned crumbs

Paprika

Place 2 oysters in the deep half of one shell or custard cup; repeat to fill 12 shells. Arrange filled shells on plastic tray or paper plates. Combine remaining ingredients. Spoon mixture onto oysters. Cook in Radarange oven 4 minutes. Sprinkle with paprika and serve hot. Makes 12 appetizers (or 4 3-shell servings).

*Or use canned oysters in individual scallop shells or tiny ramekins.

Conventional Cooking:
1. *Prepare ingredients as directed. Arrange in baking pan filled with rock salt.*
2. *Bake in a hot oven, 400°, about 12 to 14 minutes.*

PEKING SPARERIBS

3 pounds spareribs, cut in finger-size pieces
1 cup orange juice
1 tablespoon soy sauce

2 teaspoons dry mustard
1 teaspoon sugar
1 jar (3½ oz.) "hot" mustard

Put ribs, with everything except prepared mustard, into a large heavy plastic bag to marinate. Refrigerate 12 hours, turning bag over several times. Arrange ribs and marinate in 2-quart oblong baking dish (they will overlap). Brush lightly with half the prepared mustard. Cover with plastic film wrap. Cook in Radarange oven 15 minutes. Turn ribs over; turn dish 180°. Brush ribs with remaining prepared mustard. Bake 10 minutes longer in oven. Makes about 12 appetizer servings.

Conventional Cooking:
1. *Arrange ribs in single layer in large shallow baking pan, brush with mustard.*
2. *Bake in moderate over, 375°, about 40 minutes. Turn ribs, brush with remaining mustard. Continue cooking an additional 20 to 25 minutes.*

RYE SAVORIES

8 slices bacon, partially cooked
½ pound sharp cheese
1 medium onion

2 teaspoons dry mustard
2 tablespoons mayonnaise
Party rye slices

Partially cook the bacon between layers of paper towels in the Radarange oven 4 to 5 minutes. Put bacon, cheese, and onion through fine blade of food grinder. Blend in mustard and mayonnaise. Spread thinly on slices of party rye; arrange

on paper plates or trays. Heat in oven 35 to 40 seconds.
Makes about 2 cups, enough for 4 to 5 dozen savories.

Conventional Cooking:
1. *On cookie sheet, arrange spread rye slices in single layer.*
2. *Bake in moderate oven, 350°, about 4 to 5 minutes, until hot and bubbly.*

SALMON AND EGG APPETIZER

4 tablespoons butter or margarine	⅛ teaspoon freshly ground black pepper
¼ pound smoked salmon, chopped	6 medium eggs, beaten
¼ cup minced onion	2–3 tablespoons chopped parsley

Heat butter in 8-inch-square glass dish in Radarange oven
for 30 seconds. Add salmon, onion, and pepper; cook in oven
2 minutes. Mix in beaten eggs. Cook 1 minute. Stir; turn dish
¼ turn, cook 2 minutes; turn dish ¼ turn, cook 2 minutes.
Let stand 8 to 10 minutes. Sprinkle with parsley, cut in 1-
inch squares to serve. Makes 25 squares.

Conventional Cooking:
1. *Prepare as directed.*
2. *Bake in a slow moderate oven, 325°, about 25 minutes or until egg mixture is set.*

SARDINE CANAPÉS

1 tablespoon butter or margarine	4 stuffed olives, minced
1 tablespoon flour	1 teaspoon capers, chopped
¼ cup milk	1 can (4 oz.) sardines, drained and chopped
⅓ cup mayonnaise	Unsalted crisp crackers
1 teaspoon lemon juice	Paprika

Measure butter into a small bowl; heat in Radarange oven 45 seconds. Blend in flour. Gradually add milk, stirring until smooth. Cook in oven 30 seconds; stir; cook 15 seconds. Cool. Mix together with all remaining ingredients except crackers. Chill until thick. Spread crackers with mixture, using about ½ teaspoonful per cracker. Arrange 12 crackers on a flat plate or paper towels; heat in oven 30 to 45 seconds. Repeat with remaining crackers. Sprinkle with paprika. Serve hot. Makes 2 dozen canapés.

Conventional Cooking:
1. *Prepare as directed. Arrange spread crackers on cookie sheet.*
2. *Bake in hot oven, 400°, for 7 to 8 minutes.*

SHRIMP IN BEER

1 can (12 oz.) beer	⅛ teaspoon Tabasco sauce
½ lemon, juice and peel	1 pound frozen ready-to-
1 tablespoon mixed pickling	cook shrimp, defrosted
spices	
½ teaspoon celery seed,	
crushed	

Mix beer, lemon, and seasonings in a bowl. Heat in Radarange oven 2 minutes, or to a bubble. Add shrimp; cook 3 minutes. Cool and chill shrimp in liquid. When ready to serve, remove shrimp to chilled serving dish. Serve with sauce for dipping. Makes 8 appetizer servings.

Sauce:

1 tablespoon flour	2 tablespoons chili sauce
½ cup reserved shrimp	1 tablespoon prepared
marinade, strained	horseradish

Blend flour into liquid; cook in Radarange oven 1 minute; stir well to remove lumps. Cook 30 seconds more. Stir in remaining ingredients. Serve warm or cold as a dip for shrimp. Makes about ¾ cup.

Conventional Cooking:
1. *Cook shrimp in beer marinade over moderate heat until pink, about 5 to 6 minutes. Cool and chill in cooking liquid.*
2. *Mix sauce ingredients in small saucepan. Cook and stir over moderate heat until thickened.*

SPINACH TARTLET

2 cups firmly packed shredded fresh spinach
3 tablespoons chopped onion
¼ teaspoon basil, crumbled
3 tablespoons butter or margarine
¼ pound fresh mushrooms, sliced
1 tablespoon flour

1 cup shredded natural Swiss cheese
1 cup whipping cream
4 medium eggs, beaten
Pinch nutmeg
Dash cayenne pepper
¼ teaspoon black pepper
1 teaspoon salt (or to taste)
Paprika

Mix together spinach, onion, and basil; cook in Radarange oven 1 minute. Turn into electric blender container; blend until smooth. Heat butter or margarine in 10″ glass pie plate in oven 45 seconds. Add sliced mushrooms; cook 1 minute. Sprinkle with flour, stir, cook 1 minute. Spoon the spinach puree on top of mushrooms; sprinkle with cheese. Beat remaining ingredients together with wire wisk; pour over cheese. Cook in oven 10 to 12 minutes, giving plate a quarter turn every 3 minutes. After 6 minutes of cooking time spoon some of uncooked portion from center over the top. Remove from oven; let stand 10 minutes. Sprinkle with paprika. Cut in wedges to serve. Makes 10 to 12 appetizer servings.

Conventional Cooking:
1. *Prepare as above, cooking on top of stove over moderate heat.*
2. *Bake in slow moderate oven, 325°, about 50 to 55 minutes until set.*

SWISS FONDUE

1 clove garlic	2 tablespoons cornstarch
1½ cups dry white wine	3 tablespoons brandy
1 pound natural Gruyere cheese, grated	Black pepper
	Pinch thyme

Rub the bottom and sides of a 1½-quart glass or ceramic casserole with garlic. Add wine; heat in Radarange oven 2 minutes. Add cheese dredged in cornstarch; cook in oven 4 to 5 minutes, or until cheese is melted, stirring every 2 minutes. Stir in brandy and seasonings. Serve hot with cubes of French bread for dipping. Makes fondue for 4 to 6.

Conventional Cooking:

1. *Prepare and mix together ingredients as directed. Heat over low heat until cheese melts, about 18 to 20 minutes.*
2. *Stir until creamy. Stir in brandy and seasonings. Reheat as mixture gets cold and stiffens.*

TERIYAKI STRIPS

1 pound sirloin tip, cut about ¼" thick	¼ cup sherry
½ teaspoon ginger	Party rye slices
½ cup bottled teriyaki sauce	

Cut beef into thin strips across the grain. Mix together ginger, sauce, and sherry, pour over meat. Let stand in refrigerator 1 hour, turning meat several times; drain. Thread meat strips on bamboo skewers; arrange around edge of shallow baking dish. Cook in Radarange oven 2 minutes, or until steak is done to taste. Push meat off skewers; serve hot with buttered slices of party rye bread. Makes about 3 dozen strips.

Rare . . . Cook in oven 1 minute. Turn skewers and turn dish 180°. Cook 1 minute.
Medium to well . . . Cook in oven 1 minute. Turn skewers, turn dish 180°. Cook 1½ to 2½ minutes.

Conventional Cooking:
1. *Heat a heavy fry pan, brush with a little oil. Quickly sear meat strips over high heat. Mix and turn to prevent overcooking.*
2. *Serve as above.*

TIPSY STUFFED EGGS

2 tablespoons butter or margarine
½ cup finely chopped fresh mushrooms
2 tablespoons minced onion
1 tablespoon chopped parsley
Dash Tabasco sauce
⅛ teaspoon seasoned pepper

6 large hard-cooked eggs, halved
2–3 tablespoons light rum
4 anchovy fillets, finely minced
Buttered Bread Crumbs (page 223)
12 toast rounds, buttered

Heat butter in Radarange oven 20 seconds. Stir in mushrooms, onion, parsley, and seasonings; cook 1½ minutes. Add mashed egg yolks, rum, and anchovies. Stuff egg whites with anchovy mixture, sprinkle with buttered crumbs; place each half on toast round. Arrange six on paper plates; heat in oven 30 seconds, turn dish 180°, cook 30 seconds more. Repeat with remaining eggs. Serve hot. Makes 12 appetizers.

Conventional Cooking:

1. *Hard cook eggs, cool, halve, and remove yolks. Sauté mushrooms, onion, parsley and seasonings in hot butter. Mash with egg yolks, rum, and anchovies. Fill egg white halves with mixture, sprinkle with crumbs.*
2. *Arrange on cookie sheet, or shallow baking pan. Heat in slow oven, 325°, about 4 to 5 minutes. Serve on buttered toast rounds.*

Very Special Soups

For special soups and stews that would take a long time to cook on a conventional range, the microwave oven will delight you with its speed and the flavor that results. A hearty beef and vegetable soup will cook in 20 minutes; chick pea soup (Fassoulada) in 25 minutes. And so it goes. More soup recipes follow, and you will find recipes for stews, ragouts, and other main dishes of this type in the chapters that follow.

BEEF AND VEGETABLE SOUP

1 can (13¾ oz.) condensed beef bouillon
1 soup can water
1 pound lean ground beef
3 tablespoons cream of rice cereal
1 teaspoon salt
⅛ teaspoon pepper
⅛ teaspoon garlic powder
1 egg
½ cup chopped onion
½ cup sliced or chopped celery

1 tablespoon vegetable oil
1 tablespoon bottled browning sauce
1 can (1 lb.) whole tomatoes
1 can (1 lb.) mixed vegetables
1 can (3 or 4 oz.) sliced mushrooms, with broth
1 teaspoon parsley flakes
¼ teaspoon thyme
Grated Parmesan cheese

46

Mix bouillon and water; reserve. Mix together beef, cream of rice, seasonings, egg, and ¼ cup bouillon; shape into 3 or 4 dozen little meatballs. Cook onion and celery in oil in 4-quart baking dish in Radarange oven uncovered 3 minutes; stir once. Add 1 cup bouillon, browning sauce, and meat balls; cook covered 7 minutes, or until boiling. Stir meat balls; add remaining ingredients. Cover, cook 10 minutes, stirring once halfway through cooking time. Serve with grated Parmesan cheese. Makes about 8 servings.

Conventional Cooking:
1. *Sauté onion, celery, and meat balls in hot oil. Add remaining ingredients.*
2. *Simmer covered over low moderate heat for about 1 hour. Stir often.*

CLEAR MUSHROOM SOUP

3 tablespoons butter or margarine	1½ quarts boiling water, divide
1 onion, chopped	4 whole allspice
1 leek, chopped	3 whole cloves
1 carrot, chopped	1 bay leaf
1 stalk celery, chopped	⅛ teaspoon coarse ground black pepper
1 tomato, chopped	1 teaspoon salt
1 pound fresh mushrooms, chopped	5 bouillon cubes, crushed
1 garlic clove, chopped	½ cup dry white wine
1 slice beef marrow bone	

Mix together butter or margarine and vegetables in 4-quart casserole. Cook, covered, in the Radarange oven 5 minutes. Add bone and 2 cups boiling water. Cook covered in oven 10 minutes; stir after 5 minutes. Add remaining ingredients (except wine). Cook 10 minutes, covered. Let stand until cool; strain; chill. Discard top layer of congealed fat. Heat to a simmer. Stir in wine. Makes 5 to 6 servings.

Conventional Cooking:

1. *Sauté vegetables and butter on medium heat in large (4-quart) saucepan about 20 minutes.*
2. *Add remaining ingredients (except wine). Simmer covered about 1½ hours. Stir in wine.*

CREAMY GARDEN SOUP

2 tablespoons butter or margarine	2 cups chicken broth
¼ cup chopped onion	1 cup boiling water
1 small head lettuce, shredded (about 2 cups)	1 teaspoon seasoned salt
½ bunch watercress, chopped (about 1 cup)	Dash pepper
1 cucumber, diced	1 cup half and half
	Chives

Melt butter in 2½-quart casserole in Radarange oven 40 seconds. Add onion, cook in oven 1 minute. Add vegetables, cook 5 minutes. Process mixture in blender until smooth. Return to casserole, stir in chicken broth, boiling water, seasoning and stir in half and half. Return casserole to oven; cook covered 2 minutes or until heated through. Garnish with chopped chives. Makes 6 servings.

Conventional Cooking:

1. *Cook first 9 ingredients on top of stove about 25 minutes over medium heat. Put through blender until smooth. Return to saucepan.*
2. *Stir in half and half, cook over low heat 3 to 5 minutes until heated through.*

FASSOULADA
(Chick Pea Soup)

1 cup chopped celery (2–3
stalks)
1 cup chopped carrot (3–4
carrots)
1½ cups chopped onion
(2 medium)
¼ cup chopped parsley
⅓ cup olive oil

1 can (1 lb.) chick peas
(drained and washed)
¼ cup catchup
⅛ teaspoon black pepper
1 teaspoon salt (or to taste)
1 quart boiling water
5 beef bouillon cubes,
crushed

Mix together the vegetables and olive oil in a large (2½-quart) casserole. Cook, covered, in Radarange oven 15 minutes, stirring every 5 minutes. Add chick peas, seasonings, boiling water, and bouillon cubes. Mix together well. Cook, covered, in oven 10 minutes; stir once. Makes 4 to 5 generous servings.

Conventional Cooking:
1. Combine ingredients in a large kettle.
2. Cook over medium heat about 1 hour.

FRESH WATERCRESS CREAM SOUP

2 tablespoons butter or margarine
2 tablespoons flour
3 cups watercress (packed)
3 cans (10½ oz. each) condensed beef broth

⅛ teaspoon black pepper
1 cup whipping cream
Grated Parmesan cheese

Melt butter in Radarange oven 30 seconds. Mix together butter, flour, watercress, and broth. Process mixture (½ amount at a time) in electric blender until very smooth (about 1 minute). Pour into 2½-quart casserole, cook covered in oven 4 minutes. Stir in pepper and cream. Cover, return to oven for 3 minutes to reheat. Serve hot with a garnish of grated Parmesan cheese. Makes 6 servings.

Conventional Cooking:
1. *Process ingredients in blender as directed. Turn into sauce-pan and simmer covered over medium heat until thickened, about 20 minutes.*
2. *Stir in cream, heat a minute or 2. Serve hot.*

GARDEN PATCH BORSCHT

2 onions, chopped
1 large potato, chopped
3 cups shredded red cab-bage
1 large ripe tomato, peeled and chopped
2 (1 lb.) cans whole beets grated, or 2 lbs. fresh*
3 tablespoons vegetable oil

3 cups boiling water
½ teaspoon dill seed, crushed
2 bay leaves, crumbled
3 to 4 whole allspice
1 teaspoon salt
⅓ cup mild vinegar
2 cups strong beef broth
Dash sugar, to taste

Mix together all vegetables (except beets) with oil in a 4-quart casserole. Cover and cook in Radarange oven 7 minutes; stir, cook 7 minutes more. Add remaining ingredients, include grated beets; cook in oven, covered, for 10 minutes. Let stand, covered, 10 minutes before serving. Makes 8 servings.

*If fresh beets are used instead of canned, add when vegetables are cooked in oil.

Conventional Cooking:
1. *Mix together all ingredients, stir well and bring to a boil.*
2. *Reduce heat to a simmer; cook about 2 hours, stirring occasionally. Adjust seasoning before serving.*

GUATEMALAN BREAD SOUP

6 slices firm white bread,
toasted
4 tablespoons butter or
margarine, divided
1 cup chopped onion
1 can (1 lb.) stewed
tomatoes

2 tablespoons flour
¼ teaspoon pepper
1 cup water
6 cups hot chicken bouillon
or broth
2 hard cooked eggs, sliced
Grated Parmesan cheese

Spread toast with 3 tablespoons butter; set aside to be used later. Sauté remaining butter and onions in 3- to 4-quart casserole in Radarange oven 3 minutes; stir. Add stewed tomatoes. Cook 2 minutes longer. Mix flour and pepper to a smooth paste with a little of the water. Stir into tomato mixture with remaining water. Cook in oven 6 minutes until thickened. Stir after 3 minutes of cooking time. Stir in hot bouillon; cook 2 minutes longer until very hot. To serve, top each portion with 1 slice of buttered toast cut in ½-inch strips. Garnish with egg slices and cheese. Makes 6 to 8 servings.

Conventional Cooking:
1. Prepare and mix ingredients as directed.
2. Cook over medium heat about 45 to 50 minutes. Top with toast strips, egg, and cheese.

ICED FRESH TOMATO SOUP

2 tablespoons vegetable oil
4 small onions, chopped
2 pounds fresh ripe toma-
toes, chopped (about 6
medium)
1 can (10½ oz.) condensed
beef broth
¼ cup catchup

2 tablespoons finely chopped
fresh dill or 1 tablespoon
dry dill weed
1 teaspoon salt
Dash Tabasco sauce
3 cups crushed ice
½ cup whipping cream

Heat oil in 2½-quart casserole in Radarange oven 1½ minutes. Add onions and tomatoes; cook 4 minutes. Stir in broth and catchup; cover, cook in oven 2 minutes. Process in blender until very smooth. Return mixture to casserole. Stir in remaining ingredients (except cream). Chill until very cold, about 4 hours. Whip cream until it stands in soft peaks. If desired, season with ¼ teaspoon curry powder. Before serving, blend soup with rotary beater. Garnish with whipped cream. Makes 6 servings.

Conventional Cooking:
1. *Cook onions and tomatoes in oil for few minutes; do not brown. Stir in broth and catchup; cook about 10 minutes.*
2. *Process in blender until smooth. Stir in seasonings and ice. Chill. Beat smooth and serve with whipped cream.*

ITALIAN ZUCCHINI SOUP

2 tablespoons olive oil
4 cups finely chopped
  zucchini
3 scallions, chopped
1 clove garlic, minced
2 teaspoons salt
⅛ teaspoon pepper

½ teaspoon basil
4 cups beef broth
2 tablespoons minced
  parsley
1 tablespoon butter
Grated Parmesan cheese

Mix together oil, zucchini, scallions, and garlic in a 2½- to 3-quart casserole. Cover, cook in Radarange oven 10 minutes; stir once. Add seasonings and broth; cover, cook in oven 5 minutes. Stir in parsley and butter. Serve with cheese. Makes 4 to 5 servings.

Conventional Cooking:
1. *Use a large kettle. Cook first 4 ingredients together about 10 minutes. Add remaining ingredients except cheese.*
2. *Cook covered over medium heat about 35 minutes. Serve with cheese.*

MINESTRONE

3 tablespoons olive oil
1 garlic clove, minced
1 onion, minced
1 tablespoon minced parsley
1 medium potato, finely
  diced
1 cup finely shredded
  cabbage
1 cup finely chopped celery
1 cup finely chopped carrots

1 cup chopped spinach
1 can (10½ oz.) condensed
  beef broth
2 cups boiling water
½ cup canned garbanzo
  beans (chick peas)
1 can (8 oz.) tomato sauce
1 teaspoon salt
Dash pepper
Parmesan cheese, grated

Mix together oil and next 7 ingredients in 3- to 4-quart casserole. Cook, covered, in Radarange oven 7 minutes. Stir, cook covered 7 minutes more. Add remaining ingredients, except cheese. Cover, cook in oven 10 minutes. Stir, let stand covered 10 minutes before serving. Serve with grated Parmesan cheese. Makes 6 to 8 servings.

Conventional Cooking:
1. *Sauté garlic, onion, parsley, and potato in hot olive oil in large kettle. Stir in remaining ingredients.*
2. *Cook covered over medium heat about 1 hour, until very thick.*

MONTEREY MÉLANGE

2 tablespoons butter or
  margarine
1 small onion, chopped
1 small green pepper, diced
3 medium tomatoes, peeled
  and diced
1 can (1 lb. 14 oz.) red kidney beans, drained

2 tablespoons chili powder
½ teaspoon salt
Dash pepper
Dash Tabasco sauce
½ pound sharp cheddar
  cheese, grated
4 slices bacon, cooked and
  crumbled (page 75)

Melt butter in 2- to 2½-quart casserole in Radarange oven 1 minute. Add onion, pepper, and tomatoes; cook 4 minutes. Add beans, seasonings, and cheese; mix well. Cook in oven, covered, 7 minutes, stirring halfway through cooking time. Sprinkle with crumbled bacon before serving. Makes 6 to 8 servings.

Conventional Cooking:
1. *Sauté vegetables in butter in heavy fry pan. Stir in remaining ingredients (except bacon).*
2. *Cook and stir over low heat (simmer) until cheese melts and mixture is heated through; about 20 minutes. Sprinkle with crumbled bacon.*

NATURAL BARLEY SOUP

¼ cup whole quick barley, rinsed

2 tablespoons butter or margarine

1 quart beef broth

1 quart water

1 cup sliced celery (2 stalks)

1 cup sliced carrots (2 medium carrots)

¼ cup chopped onion

1 can (1 lb.) tomatoes, chopped

1 cup fresh peas

Salt and pepper to taste

Parsley, chopped

Mix together barley, butter, and vegetables in a large (3- to 4-quart) casserole. Cover, cook in Radarange oven 10 minutes, stir halfway through cooking time. Add remaining ingredients, mix well, cook covered 30 minutes; stir once. Sprinkle with parsley; serve hot. Makes 6 to 8 servings.

Conventional Cooking:
1. *Combine ingredients in a large kettle. Bring to a boil, then reduce heat to a simmer.*
2. *Cook covered over low heat about 1½ hours.*

ONE-OF-A-KIND SOUP

1 medium potato, peeled and finely chopped
1 medium onion, finely chopped
1 cucumber, peeled and chopped
2 stalks celery, chopped
1 tart apple, peeled and chopped

1 tablespoon butter or margarine
4 cups hot chicken broth
1 cup light cream
1 teaspoon curry powder
Pinch white pepper
1 teaspoon salt (or to taste)
Chives

Mix together chopped vegetables, apple, and butter in a 3- to 4-quart casserole. Cook covered in Radarange oven 10 minutes; stir halfway through cooking time. Add hot broth, cook 10 minutes more, covered. Let cool; blend in electric blender until smooth. Stir in cream and seasonings. Chill. Serve very cold. Sprinkle with chopped chives. Makes 6 servings.

Conventional Cooking:
1. Combine ingredients except cream in large saucepan. Cover, cook over medium heat about 35 minutes. Cool slightly.
2. Process in blender until smooth. Stir in cream. Chill. Serve very cold.

VICHYSSOISE

4 leeks, finely chopped
3 cups diced raw potatoes
3 cups boiling water
1 tablespoon butter or margarine
3 chicken bouillon cubes, crushed

1 cup whipping cream
1 cup milk
2 teaspoons salt
¼ teaspoon pepper
2 tablespoons cut chives

Mix together leeks, potatoes and water in 2½-quart casserole. Cover, cook in Radarange oven 15 minutes. Stir in butter and crushed bouillon cubes. Process in blender until very smooth. Return to casserole, stir in cream, milk, and seasonings. Cover, cook in oven 3 to 4 minutes. Serve hot or chilled, garnished with chives. Makes 5 to 6 servings.

Conventional Cooking:
1. *Cook vegetables with water, covered, until very soft. Add butter and bouillon cubes; process in blender until smooth.*
2. *Stir in cream, milk, and seasonings. Heat to a simmer. Garnish with chives.*

Chowders

A hearty chowder, brimming with satisfying flavor and nourishment, is a meal in itself, needing only a green salad and a simple dessert to round it out. The savory aroma that rises as the chowder is ladled into serving bowls will bring the family to the table on the run, and they will not be disappointed as they dip and sip! Among other delights in this section you'll find Captain's Chowder, Spanish Bean Chowder, and Cheese Chowder—every one a taste treat.

CAPTAIN'S CHOWDER

4 slices bacon, cooked and crumbled (page 75)
2 tablespoons bacon fat
1 medium onion, finely chopped
1 small green pepper, finely chopped
1 canned pimiento, chopped
1 can (4 oz.) mushroom stems and pieces, drained

1 can (10¾ oz.) condensed cream of potato soup
1 soup can milk
1 can (7 oz.) tuna, drained and flaked
Salt and pepper to taste
Mace (optional)

Cook bacon; drain, reserving fat. Measure 2 tablespoons bacon fat into 2½-quart casserole, stir in onion, pepper, and pimiento. Cook in Radarange oven 4 minutes. Add mushrooms, soup, and milk. Mix well; cover, cook in oven 5 minutes. Add tuna and bacon. Cover, cook in oven 2 to 3 minutes until very hot. Stir, add salt and pepper to taste, dash with mace before serving. Makes 4 servings.

Conventional Cooking:
1. *Prepare bacon as directed. Sauté onion, pepper, and pimiento in bacon fat in large saucepan. Add remaining ingredients. Cook over medium heat covered about 30 minutes.*
2. *Add bacon, cook and stir 3 to 4 minutes.*

CHEESE CHOWDER

3 tablespoons butter or margarine	*¼ cup flour*
¼ cup finely chopped onion	*½ teaspoon salt*
½ cup finely chopped carrot	*3 cups milk*
½ cup finely chopped celery	*2 cups chicken broth*
	1 cup grated sharp process cheese
	Paprika

Melt butter in 2½-quart casserole in Radarange oven 30 seconds. Stir in onion, celery, and carrots. Cook 5 minutes; stir once. Blend in flour and salt. Gradually add milk, stirring constantly. Cover, cook in oven 3 minutes, stir; cook 2 minutes more. Add chicken broth and cheese. Cover, cook 5 minutes, stirring once. Sprinkle with paprika before serving. Makes 6 servings.

Conventional Cooking:
1. *Cook onion in butter few minutes, do not brown. Add flour and milk to make a thin white sauce. Cook 5 minutes or so. Add remaining ingredients; simmer over low heat, covered, about 35 minutes.*
2. *Stir in cheese; simmer about 10 minutes.*

HAMBURGER CHOWDER

1½ pounds ground beef
3 medium onions, finely
    chopped
3 small carrots, finely
    chopped
3 small potatoes, finely
    chopped
3 stalks celery, diced
2 quarts hot water
4 beef bouillon cubes

1 can (1 lb.) tomatoes
½ cup quick cooking barley
1 tablespoon salt (or to
    taste)
⅛ teaspoon pepper
Pinch thyme
⅓ cup flour
1 cup cooked or canned
    green peas

Shape meat into thick flat patty, place in large casserole or Dutch oven. Cook in Radarange, covered, 5 minutes. Let stand, covered, while vegetables cook. Cook onions, carrots, potatoes, and celery in 4-quart covered casserole 5 minutes; stir, cook 5 minutes more. Add ground beef broken up with a fork, and remaining ingredients (except flour and peas). Cover; cook 15 minutes. Drain liquid from peas, mix with flour till smooth. Stir in hot soup. Add peas. Cover and cook in oven 10 minutes more. Stir well, let stand few minutes before serving. Makes 10 servings.

Conventional Cooking:
1. *Sauté beef in Dutch oven. Add ingredients as directed. Cover, cook over medium heat about 1 hour. Thicken with flour paste.*
2. *Continue to cook over low heat about 20 minutes; add peas.*

QUICK SUPPER CHOWDER

6 slices bacon, cooked crisp
  and diced (page 75)
1 cup diced cooked carrots
1 cup diced cooked potatoes
4 tablespoons butter or
  bacon drippings
1 large onion, very thinly
  sliced

1 can (1 lb.) creamed corn
1 can (10 oz.) condensed
  cream of chicken soup
2½ cups milk
Dash pepper
Salt to taste

Prepare bacon and set aside. To cook diced carrots and potatoes, mix and cook in medium-size cooking bag or small casserole. Cook, covered, 5 minutes. Heat butter or drippings in 2-quart casserole in Radarange oven 45 seconds. Add onion separated into rings; cook 2 minutes, stir, cook 2 minutes more. Stir in remaining ingredients. Mix together well. Cover; cook in oven 5 minutes. Stir well and cook 5 minutes more till soup is hot. Sprinkle with diced bacon before serving. Makes 6 servings.

Conventional Cooking:
1. Sauté onion in bacon drippings in heavy kettle. Mix in remaining ingredients.
2. Simmer over low medium heat about 35 to 40 minutes.

SPANISH BEAN CHOWDER

2 small onions, sliced
1 garlic clove, minced
3 medium potatoes, finely
   diced
1 tablespoon olive oil
1 teaspoon salt
Dash Tabasco sauce
½ teaspoon oregano
1 teaspoon sugar
2 tablespoons lemon juice

1 can (1 lb.) tomatoes,
   broken up
4 cups boiling water
1 can (1 lb. 14 oz.) red
   kidney beans
2 cups finely shredded
   cabbage
1 cup elbow macaroni,
   uncooked

Mix together first 9 ingredients in large (4-quart) casserole. Cook, covered, in Radarange oven 10 minutes, stirring after 5 minutes. Add remaining ingredients; cover, cook in oven 20 minutes; stir after 10 minutes. Let stand 5 to 10 minutes, covered, before serving. Makes 8–10 servings.

Conventional Cooking:
1. Combine first 11 ingredients in large kettle. Cook over medium heat about 1 hour.
2. Add beans, cabbage, and macaroni. Continue to cook about 30 minutes until macaroni is cooked and chowder is very thick.

CHAPTER 2:

Main Dishes—Family Style, Party Style

Casseroles

Some of the most delightful dishes ever served can never be duplicated! They were created by a cook and a casserole, using foods discovered in the refrigerator plus a savory sauce! There's nothing like a casserole to stimulate creative cooking.

Casseroles may be prepared ahead of time and kept in the freezer until you are ready to use them. Main dish casseroles are a wonderful basis for buffet entertaining. Meats, fish, seafoods, and vegetables can all be used to create simple or elegant casseroles. They can be prepared

61

ahead of time and left in the refrigerator for other members of the family to cook if you cannot be at home at the dinner hour.

The group of recipes that follows will get you off to a good creative start.

EASY CHICKEN CASSEROLE

2 cups dry bread cubes
2 cups cooked chicken, diced
2 tablespoons parsley, chopped

1½ teaspoons seasoning salt
¼ teaspoon pepper
2 eggs, beaten
1 cup chicken broth
1 cup milk

Mix bread cubes and chicken in 2-quart glass casserole: stir in remaining ingredients. Bake in Radarange oven 12 minutes, gently stirring every 4 minutes of cooking time. Makes 4 servings.

Conventional Cooking:
1. *Combine ingredients as directed, turn into casserole.*
2. *Bake in moderate oven, 350°, 35 to 40 minutes.*

FISH 'N' CHIPS CASSEROLE

1 can (10¾ oz.) condensed cream of celery soup
⅓ cup light cream
1 can (3 oz.) sliced broiled mushrooms with broth

1 bag (2 oz.) potato chips, crushed
1 can (7 oz.) tuna, drained

Mix together soup, cream, and mushrooms with broth. Arrange layers of crushed chips, flaked tuna, and soup mixture in 1-quart casserole, beginning and ending with crushed chips. Cook in Radarange oven 8 minutes, turning dish a quarter turn 2 times. Makes 4 servings.

Conventional Cooking:
1. *Prepare ingredients and layer into small casserole.*
2. *Bake in moderate oven, 375°, about 30 to 35 minutes.*

HAMBURGER "STEW" EN CASSEROLE

1½ pounds lean ground
  beef
1 teaspoon salt
Dash pepper
1 large onion, chopped
1 tablespoon oil
¼ teaspoon oregano
1 can (1 lb.) tomatoes

1 can (8 oz.) sliced carrots,
  drained
1 cup cooked potatoes,
  diced
1 cup water or broth
3 tablespoons flour
1 packet (¾ oz.) dry Italian
  salad dressing mix

Mix beef with seasonings; shape into small balls. Mix onion and oil in 10-inch ceramic skillet. Cook in Radarange oven 1½ minutes; stir, cook 1½ minutes more. Arrange meat balls in a single layer in 2-quart oblong baking dish; cover with paper towels. Cook 5 minutes; turn dish, cook 3 to 5 minutes more. Drain meatballs, add to cooked onions in skillet and add tomatoes and vegetables. Mix together water or broth, flour, and salad dressing mix, and stir into skillet. Cover, cook in oven 5 minutes. Stir well; cook uncovered in oven 3 to 4 minutes more. Makes 6 servings.

Conventional Cooking:
1. *Prepare ingredients as indicated. Turn into casserole.*
2. *Bake covered in moderate oven, 350°, 45 to 50 minutes.*

HAWAIIAN STYLE SHRIMP CURRY

6 tablespoons butter or
  margarine
1 small onion, minced
¼ cup flour
1 teaspoon curry powder, or
  to taste
1 cup milk

1 cup coconut milk
1 tablespoon grated green
  ginger root or ½ tea-
  spoon powdered ginger
2 teaspoons lemon juice
1 pound fresh shrimp,
  shelled and deveined

Place butter and onion in 2½-quart casserole, cook in
Radarange oven 2 minutes. Stir in flour and curry powder to
make a smooth paste. Add both milks; stir. Cook in oven
1½ minutes; stir well. Cook in oven 2 minutes more, stirring
every minute. Add remaining ingredients, mix well. Cook in
oven 4 minutes, stirring once. Serve with fluffy rice and toasted
flaked coconut. Makes 4 servings.

Conventional Cooking:
1. *Make sauce as indicated. Add shrimp to hot sauce.*
2. *Cook and stir over medium heat until shrimp is tender
   and pink, about 12 to 15 minutes.*

HEARTY GERMAN SUPPER

1 can or jar (1 lb.)
  applesauce
1 can (14 oz.) sauerkraut,
  drained and chopped
⅓ cup dry white wine
2 tablespoons brown sugar
1 can (1 lb.) small white
  potatoes, drained

1 can (1 lb.) whole onions,
  drained
1 ring (12 oz.) Polish sausage, slashed 5 to 6 times
Parsley

The Amana Radarange® Microwave Oven is a handsome appliance that can be placed almost anywhere in the kitchen —on a counter, on a cart, or built in with a special kit. It produces so little heat that there is no fear of damaging the surroundings. Even plants may be kept in close proximity. Almost no work is involved in keeping it so bright and shining that it retains its new look inside and out, however much it is used.

When you cook with a Radarange oven, you will soon discover how much time it saves, how much of your energy it conserves, what beautiful results it produces, and how much fun it is to use.

The oven is cool: the food in the casserole is piping hot and ready to serve, and the baking dish is only warm from the heat of the food within. Kitchen magic is the name for Radarange oven cooking!

Above, Hot Seashore Dip (page 35). On the left, Chocolate Applesauce Nut Cake (page 191), Apricot Baked Chicken (page 111), Cornish Cassoulet (page 114), Orange Glazed Pork Roast (page 92), and Vegetable Special (page 186).

Polynesian Medley (above) is a beautiful main dish for a dinner party — colorful, fragrant, exotic. You will find the recipe on page 68, and a menu using it on page 240.

Fresh Watercress Cream Soup (page 49) is an enticing first course and makes a fine twosome when teamed with a salad in the ever popular soup and salad meal for luncheon or supper.

Mix together applesauce, sauerkraut, wine, and brown sugar in 2-quart baking dish; mix well. Cover, cook in oven 5 minutes; stir after 2½ minutes. Mix well; arrange potatoes and onions around outside edge of dish. Place sausage in center, cover, cook 8 to 10 minutes. Turn dish twice, one-quarter turn, during this period. Remove from oven; let stand, covered, 5 minutes. Sprinkle snipped parsley over top. Makes 6 servings.

Conventional Cooking:
1. *Combine ingredients as indicated.*
2. *Bake in moderate oven, 350°, 45 to 50 minutes.*

MACARONI AND FRANKFURTER CASSEROLE

1 package (8 oz.) elbow macaroni, cooked (page 221) and drained
2 cups sharp cheese, grated
1 tall can (14½ oz.) evaporated milk

1 small onion, minced
Dash pepper
10 frankfurters

Place cooked macaroni in 2- to 2½-quart casserole. Mix together, cheese, milk, onion, and pepper; stir into macaroni. Slice each frankfurter crosswise into 1″ pieces; add to macaroni mixture. Cover, cook in Radarange oven 6 minutes, stirring the macaroni after 3 minutes of cooking time. Makes 6 servings.

Conventional Cooking:
1. *Prepare and combine ingredients in casserole.*
2. *Bake in moderate oven, 350°, 40 to 45 minutes.*

MACARONI MILANO

2 tablespoons olive oil
1 onion, minced
1 garlic clove, minced
1 can (1 lb.) stewed
  tomatoes
1 can (3 oz.) tomato paste
1 bay leaf
⅛ teaspoon each thyme and
  oregano

1 teaspoon salt
Dash pepper
Dash Tabasco sauce
¾ cup diced cooked ham
1 cup cooked or canned
  chicken, diced
1 pound elbow macaroni,
  cooked (page 221) and
  drained

Heat Browning Skillet in Radarange oven 2½ minutes. Add oil, onion, and garlic; cook in oven 2 minutes. Stir in tomatoes, tomato paste, and seasonings; cook uncovered, in oven 7 to 8 minutes; stir several times. Add ham and chicken; cook in oven 1 minute. Stir in cooked macaroni. Cover; cook in oven 3 to 4 minutes. Serve with grated Parmesan cheese. Makes 6 servings.

Conventional Cooking:
1. Heat pan with oil. Sauté onion and garlic. Add sauce ingredients and cook about 10 to 15 minutes. Add remaining ingredients.
2. Cover, simmer and stir over low heat until very hot, about 10 minutes.

ORIENTAL SHRIMP

1 clove garlic, crushed
½ teaspoon grated ginger
    root
¼ cup vegetable oil, divided
12-ounce bag frozen ready-
    to-cook shrimp, thawed
1 cup diagonally sliced
    celery
1 medium onion, sliced
1 green pepper, cubed
1 can (8 oz.) tomato sauce

1 tablespoon sugar
¼ teaspoon salt
½ teaspoon MSG
    (optional)
1½ tablespoons cornstarch
¼ cup soy sauce
½ cup hot strong chicken
    broth
2 firm ripe tomatoes, cut in
    eighths

Add garlic, ginger, and 2 tablespoons oil to Browning
Skillet. Heat in Radarange oven 4 minutes. Remove garlic.
Stir in shrimp; cook in oven 2 minutes. Remove shrimp to
warm dish. Add remaining oil to Browning Skillet. Heat 2½
minutes. Stir in celery, onion, and green pepper. Cook 4
minutes, stirring twice. Return shrimp, mix well, cook 1
minute. Mix together tomato sauce, seasonings, corn starch,
soy sauce, and chicken broth. Stir sauce into shrimp mixture.
Mix well, cover, cook 4 minutes, stirring once. Add tomatoes,
cook 1 minute. Serve with hot rice or fine noodles. Makes 4
servings.

Conventional Cooking:
1. Use pan on top of stove, and cook as directed until shrimp
   is pink. Add sauce.
2. Continue to cook and stir over moderate heat until thickened, about 15 to 20 minutes.

POLYNESIAN MEDLEY

2 tablespoons butter or
   margarine
1 pound chicken livers,
   halved
1 pound ground beef
1 egg, beaten
¼ cup packaged seasoned
   bread crumbs
2 tablespoons milk
⅛ teaspoon nutmeg
½ pound cocktail
   frankfurters

1 can (1 lb.) pineapple tidbits, drained; reserve
   syrup
¼ cup brown sugar
2 tablespoons cornstarch
1 teaspoon chicken bouillon
   powder
3 tablespoons vinegar
1 tablespoon soy sauce

Heat large Browning Skillet in Radarange oven 4 minutes.
Add butter and chicken livers; stir around in hot skillet. Cover,
cook 1½ minutes; stir well, and cook 1½ minutes more.

Thoroughly mix together next 6 ingredients, shape into 1-
inch meatballs. Place in one layer in 2-quart utility dish. Cook
in oven 6 to 7 minutes, turning the dish 180° after 3 minutes
of cooking. Drain meatballs.

Remove livers from skillet. Drain pineapple, mix syrup and
remaining ingredients (except frankfurters) in Browning
Skillet. Cook in oven 3 minutes until thickened, stir twice.

To arrange meat for serving: put liver in center of shallow
3-quart casserole. Divide meatballs and place around livers
in 3 piles. Arrange frankfurters and drained pineapple tidbits
in piles between meatballs. Pour the thickened sauce over
contents of casserole. Cool, cover, refrigerate until ready to
serve. At serving time, uncover; cook in oven 13½ minutes.
Turn dish every 5 minutes. Serve in same dish. Makes 8
servings.

Conventional Cooking:
1. Sauté chicken livers, meatballs, pineapple chunks, and
   frankfurters separately. Arrange in shallow casserole as
   directed. Prepare sauce and pour over ingredients.
2. Bake in moderate oven, 350°, about 35 to 40 minutes.

68

SALMON AND GREEN BEAN CASSEROLE

1 package (9 oz.) frozen
Italian green beans
1 package (8 oz.) frozen
artichoke hearts
1 can (1 lb.) salmon,
drained
½ cup canned Hollandaise
sauce

⅓ cup dairy sour cream
½ teaspoon lemon peel,
grated
¼ teaspoon crushed
tarragon
⅛ teaspoon pepper
2 tablespoons slivered
toasted almonds

Cook frozen beans (see chart, page 154). Cook artichoke hearts in covered casserole for 5½ minutes, drain. Remove skin and bones from salmon, break into chunks. Mix together vegetables and salmon; spoon into 4 buttered individual ramekins or casseroles. Blend Hollandaise, sour cream, lemon, and seasonings. Spoon ¼ of sauce mixture into each casserole and spread over surface. Sprinkle with almonds. Cook in oven 7 to 8 minutes* until heated through. Makes 4 servings.

*If desired, casseroles may be cooked 1 at a time; allow 2 minutes per casserole.

Conventional Cooking:
1. Prepare and mix ingredients as indicated, divide mixture among 4 individual casseroles.
2. Bake in a moderate oven, 350°, 30 to 35 minutes.

SAVORY FISH AND VEGETABLE CASSEROLE

2 pounds frozen fish fillets,
   defrosted
2 cups boiling water
½ cup chopped onion
1 bay leaf
3 to 4 whole cloves
2 cups cooked or canned
   cut green beans, drained
1 cup cooked or canned
   carrots, sliced
¼ cup butter or margarine

¼ cup flour
1 teaspoon seasoned salt
1 teaspoon pepper
⅔ cup evaporated milk
1 can (10¾ oz.) condensed
   tomato soup
½ teaspoon rosemary
3 cups hot seasoned mashed
   potatoes
½ cup sharp cheese, grated
   (optional)

Place thawed fish in 2-quart casserole. Add water and seasoning; cover with plastic wrap. Cook in Radarange oven 4 minutes. Strain stock; reserve 1½ cups. Break fish into large pieces, return to casserole with green beans and carrots. Make a white sauce with the next 5 ingredients and the 1½ cups reserved fish stock (page 127). Stir in the tomato soup and rosemary. Pour sauce over fish and vegetables in casserole. Cover, cook in oven 5 minutes, turning dish 180° after 2½ minutes. Spoon mashed potatoes in ring on top of casserole. Sprinkle with cheese if desired. Cook uncovered in oven 2 minutes. Makes 6 to 8 servings.

Conventional Cooking:
1. Prepare casserole as directed.
2. Bake in moderate oven, 350°, about 45 minutes.
3. Add mashed potatoes as directed, and brown.

TUNA SUPREME

⅓ cup butter or margarine
⅓ cup flour
1 teaspoon salt
Dash pepper
1 teaspoon paprika
¼ teaspoon crushed
   rosemary

2¾ cups milk
¼ cup dry white wine
½ cup ripe olives, sliced
2 cups cooked or canned
   white onions
1 family size (12 oz.) can
   tuna, flaked

Make a White Sauce (page 235) with first 8 ingredients in 2-quart casserole. Stir in remaining ingredients. Cook in Radarange oven 3 to 4 minutes. Serve with Green Rice (page 225). Makes 6 servings.

Conventional Cooking:
1. Prepare casserole as directed.
2. Bake in moderate oven, 350°, about 30 minutes.

Meats

Cooking meats in the Radarange microwave oven is one of the great joys of owning this appliance. Time and energy are saved, the finished meat is juicy and delicious. Just follow instructions carefully and you will not be disappointed.

Use the Amana Browning Skillet to brown small cuts of meat to perfection. Or a browning glaze can be used for rich color. Large cuts of lamb, beef, and pork will brown naturally, as will turkey and ham.

Leftover meat can be served a second time without the reheated flavor noticeable in other types of cooking. Next time you barbecue, sear some extra steaks over the coals, freeze them, and when they're needed—days or months later—finish cooking them in the Radarange oven. Delicious!

The recipes that follow will give you a lift when it comes to meal planning.

To thaw meats

Place meat on a flat dish. Heat in Radarange oven 2 minutes per pound. Let meat stand at room temperature 15 to 20 minutes. Return meat to the Radarange oven for an additional 1 minute per pound. While thawing, turn meat over several times.

Sign of thawing in meats: color change in meat or fat, collection of juice in dish. Meat becomes soft and warm.

If meat is not thoroughly defrosted, add a few minutes to the total cooking time.

When thawing ground beef, remove thawed portions to prevent cooking.

Thick steaks should be thawed. Under 1½ inches, cook frozen.

Cooking meat in the Radarange oven

Choose a flat glass or ceramic dish of a suitable size.

Do not salt meat before cooking: salt may toughen the outer layer of meat. Use pepper or paprika or other condiments, but add salt after cooking is completed.

To prevent spattering while cooking, cover meat lightly with a paper towel. This also acts as a baster for the juices so that less moisture will collect in the dish.

When moisture accumulates, pour off the liquid. Excessive moisture can affect cooking: the roast may be undercooked. Microwave energy is attracted by moisture and may "neglect" the roast.

Start cooking roast with fat side down. Turn it over halfway through cooking. Turn dish around at this time, too.

Meats continue to cook after removal from the Radarange oven, so allow for that. Allow a roast to stand for 15 to 20 minutes before checking temperature. To be accurate, use a meat thermometer, inserting it in the thickest part of the meat, not next to bone or fat. If more cooking is needed, remove *thermometer* (never *put thermometer in oven*) *and return the meat to the oven. After a short time, remove the roast, and check the temperature again.*

Several factors affect cooking time: the temperature of the meat before cooking (times in book are based on room temperature), the shape and size of the meat, and whether or not the meat was aged (aged meats cook more quickly).

Roasting chart

The chart below should be used as a guide to cook meats done to your preference. This chart was developed with meats cooked from room temperature. If meats have been refrigerated just prior to cooking or are still partially frozen, it will be necessary to increase cooking time accordingly.

Kind of Meat	Time per pound
Beef	
Rolled rib or rump, sirloin tip	Rare—6½ minutes
	Medium—7½ minutes
	Well-done—8½–9 minutes
Standing rib	Rare—5½ minutes
	Medium—6½ minutes
	Well-done—7½–8 minutes
Veal	
All roasts	Medium—8–8½ minutes
	Well-done—9–9½ minutes
Pork, fresh	
Loin roast	Well-done—10 minutes
Pork, cured	
Pre-cooked ham	5 minutes
Lamb	
Rolled	Well-done—9½ minutes
Bone-in shoulder	Well-done—9 minutes
Leg	Pink—6½ minutes
	Well-done—9½ minutes
Chicken	7 minutes
Turkey	7 minutes
Duck	7 minutes

A standing period is recommended for meats cooked in the Radarange oven. This will equalize temperature and firm the meat for easy carving. During this time, there will be a rise in internal temperature of about 20 degrees for an average-size roast. After standing, the temperature of a roast should correspond with that listed in the chart below.

Kind of Meat	Temperature after Standing Time
Beef	
Rare	140°
Medium	160°
Well-done	170°
Veal	170°
Pork, fresh	170°
Pork, cured	170°
Pre-cooked ham	150°
Lamb	180°
Poultry	190°

HOW TO COOK BACON

Place a double layer of paper toweling in a 9-inch-square glass cake pan. Lay bacon strips on a paper towel and cover with another towel. Cook in Radarange oven according to the following:

1 strip—1 minute, 15 seconds
2 strips—2 minutes, 20 seconds
4 strips—4 minutes

NOTE: The brand, thickness, and type of curing will all affect cooking results.

Bacon may be cooked layers at a time between paper toweling. Twelve slices of bacon (usually ½ pound) can be layered and cooked 6 minutes. If bacon is to be crisp enough to crumble, cook for 7 minutes.

BARBECUED HAMBURGER

1 large onion, chopped
1 cup diced celery
1 tablespoon butter or
  margarine
1 pound lean ground beef
1 can (10¾ oz.) condensed
  tomato soup

½ cup catchup
3 tablespoons quick-cooking
  tapioca
1½ teaspoons chili powder
2 cans (3 to 4 oz.) sliced
  mushrooms, drained

Mix together onion, celery, and butter in 2-quart casserole
and cook in Radarange oven uncovered 3 minutes; stir after
1½ minutes. Add crumbled ground beef; cook 4 minutes, stir
after 2 minutes, drain. Add remaining ingredients, cook,
uncovered, 4 minutes more. Let stand covered 5 minutes
before serving. Serve on hamburger buns. Makes 6 servings.

Conventional Cooking:
1. *Sauté onion, celery, and beef in heavy skillet. Drain. Stir
   in remaining ingredients.*
2. *Cook over medium heat about 25 minutes.*

BEEF GOULASH

2 tablespoons shortening or
  oil, divided
2½ pounds beef top round,
  floured (1-inch squares),
  divided
2 medium onions
½ garlic clove, minced
1 bay leaf
¼ teaspoon thyme

¼ teaspoon caraway seeds
1 tablespoon paprika
1 can (1 lb.) tomatoes
1 can (6 oz.) tomato paste
1½ cups water
1 packet (1 oz.) beef soup
  mix
Salt and pepper

Heat large Browning Skillet in Radarange oven 4½ minutes.
Add half the oil and half floured beef cubes. Cook in oven

2 minutes, stir after one minute. Put beef in 2½-quart covered casserole. Wipe skillet out with paper towel, heat 2½ minutes in the oven. Add the rest of the oil and floured beef. Cook 2 minutes, stir after one minute. Add to casserole dish along with remaining ingredients; season to taste. Cover; cook in oven on defrost or slow-cook cycle, 30 minutes. Stir. Cook another 30 minutes, till meat is fork tender. Makes 6 servings.

Conventional Cooking:
1. *Brown floured meat cubes in hot fat in heavy fry pan or Dutch oven. Stir in remaining ingredients. Cover.*
2. *Cook over low heat about 1½ hours.*

BEEF KABOBS

16 1-inch cubes sirloin steak
16 squares green pepper
12 large mushroom caps
8 small white onions
½ cup Italian-style bottled
  salad dressing

1 teaspoon Worcestershire
  sauce
Dash Tabasco sauce

Use 8-inch wood or bamboo skewers. Thread meat and vegetables alternately on skewers, starting and ending with a meat cube. Fill 4 skewers. Lay 4 kabobs across shallow 1½-quart baking dish. Blend remaining ingredients, brush over kabobs. Cook in oven 4 minutes. Roll kabobs over, baste; cook 1 minute for rare, 2 minutes for medium, 3 minutes for well done. Makes 2 servings.

Conventional Cooking:
1. *Arrange kabobs in shallow roasting or broiling pan. Brush with baste.*
2. *Place under preheated broiler for about 8 to 12 minutes, turning and basting several times.*

CHINESE PEPPER BEEF

1 cup hot beef broth
2 tablespoons vegetable oil, divided
1 pound beef round steak, cut in thin slices across the grain, divided
1 clove garlic, minced, divided

2 tablespoons cornstarch
1 tablespoon plus 1 teaspoon soy sauce
2 tablespoons water
1 large green pepper, cut in fine slivers
1 teaspoon finely minced green ginger

Heat beef broth in Radarange oven 1½ minutes. Set aside. Preheat large Browning Skillet in oven 4½ minutes. Add 1 tablespoon oil, half of beef and garlic. Cook 30 seconds. Stir well, cook 30 seconds more. Remove beef from skillet; set aside. Wipe skillet with paper towel, heat skillet 2 minutes. Add rest of oil, beef, and garlic. Cook 1 minute, stirring once. Add cooked beef to skillet, and beef broth. Heat one minute in oven. Mix together cornstarch, soy sauce, and water to a smooth paste; stir into skillet. Add green pepper slices and ginger. Cook in oven 3 minutes, uncovered; stir halfway through cooking time. Makes 4 servings.

Conventional Cooking:
1. Sauté beef slices, garlic, in oil in heavy fry pan. Add broth, cover, simmer 10 minutes. Mix together next 3 ingredients; stir into broth. Cook over low heat until thickened. If too thick, add a little broth or hot water.
2. Stir in green pepper and ginger, cook a minute or two. Serve with rice or noodles.

CANTONESE RIBS

½ cup soy sauce
½ cup dry sherry
½ cup lemon juice
1 teaspoon grated lemon
  peel
1½ tablespoons brown
  sugar

½ teaspoon garlic powder
¼ teaspoon ginger
4 pounds country style pork
  spareribs, cut up
1 cup orange marmalade

Use a 2-cup measure to mix together soy sauce, sherry, lemon juice, and seasonings. Mix well. Place ribs in plastic bag (on tray or shallow dish), add marinade; close bag. Let stand at room temperature 2 hours, turning bag several times. Drain ribs, reserving ½ cup marinade. Place ribs in 2-quart oblong baking dish. Bake in Radarange oven 38 minutes. Turn dish completely around after the first 10 minutes. Bake 10 minutes more. Drain off excess juices. Turn dish around again. Cook 10 minutes; add the reserved marinade to orange marmalade, baste on ribs. Turn dish and cook 8 minutes more. Makes 6 servings.

Conventional Cooking:
1. Combine marinade ingredients, pour over ribs. Let stand several hours. Drain and reserve marinade. Spread ribs in baking pan, roast in moderate oven, 350°, about 1½ hours. Drain.
2. Brush ribs with glaze, continue roasting until very tender, about 35 to 40 minutes.

CHOW MEIN WITH BEEF HEART

1 pound beef heart
2 tablespoons vinegar
2 large onions, sliced
2 cups beef broth
3 tablespoons flour
¼ cup cold water
2 tablespoons soy sauce

Salt and pepper to taste
1½ cups sliced celery
1 can (1 lb.) bean sprouts, drained
1 can (3 oz.) chow mein noodles

Remove and discard fat and tendons from heart. Cut heart in 1-inch pieces, cover with cold water, add vinegar, soak for 3 to 4 hours. Drain; place in 2½-quart casserole. Cover, cook in Radarange oven 8 minutes. Add onions and broth; cook in oven 15 minutes, stirring 3 times. Mix flour with cold water to make a paste, stir in soy sauce and seasonings. Stir into cooked mixture; add celery; cover, cook in oven 3 minutes. Add bean sprouts; cook in oven 1 minute to heat through. Serve over chow mein noodles. Makes 4 servings.

Conventional Cooking:
1. Prepare heart by soaking as directed above.
2. Bake heart at 350° (covered with onions and beef broth) 1 hour. Add rest of ingredients and bake 15 more minutes.

COUNTRY STYLE LAMB AND POTATOES

3½–4 pound half leg lamb
½ teaspoon instant minced garlic
½ teaspoon salt
1 teaspoon crushed rosemary

1 tablespoon flour
4 medium potatoes, pared and quartered (1 lb.)
⅓ cup sherry or white wine

Pierce meat all over using a pointed knife or skewer. Rub meat with seasonings mixed with flour. Place meat in baking dish (about 1½-quart), fat side down. Cook in Radarange oven 10 minutes*; turn dish 180° and cook 10 minutes more. Turn roast fat side up. Add potatoes around lamb roast. Sprinkle with any remaining seasoning mix. Pour sherry around potatoes. Cover, cook 20 minutes more; turn dish 180° halfway through cooking time. Let stand covered about 10 minutes, or until meat thermometer reaches 175–180°. Makes 6 to 8 servings.

*Lamb is cooked 9 to 9½ minutes per pound for well done.

Conventional Cooking:
1. *Prepare lamb with seasonings rubbed on roast.*
2. *Bake in 325° oven about 2 hours†. About 30 minutes before the lamb roast is done, add potatoes and sherry around the roast. Cover and finish cooking.*

†Lamb is cooked 30 to 35 minutes per pound.

DEEP DISH LAMB PIE WITH POPPY SEED CRUST

1 tablespoon poppy seeds
1 cup packaged pie crust mix
2 tablespoons water
3 pounds lamb shoulder
2 cups boiling water
⅓ cup shortening
⅛ teaspoon seasoned pepper
⅓ cup flour
1 teaspoon bottled browning sauce
1 package (10 oz.) frozen green peas and carrots, thawed
1 cup cooked or canned small white onions
Salt and pepper
Pinch crushed rosemary

Stir poppy seeds into pie crust mix; prepare pie crust as directed on package. Roll out pastry into an oblong slightly larger than top of 2-quart oblong baking pan. Cut 2 slits in middle to form a cross. Use a fork to flute edge. Place pastry on paper towels, cover with paper towels. Cook in Radarange oven 2 minutes. Remove top layer of paper towels.

Cook in oven 1 minute. Let stand while preparing remainder of pie.

Place lamb in 2- to 2½-quart casserole with boiling water. Cover, cook 24 minutes or until fork tender; turn meat over after 12 minutes. Cool. Remove meat from bones, cut into 1-inch cubes. Melt shortening in 2-quart oblong baking dish in oven 1 minute. Stir in pepper and flour to make a paste. Skim fat from broth in which lamb cooked, add enough hot water to make 3 cups liquid. Stir liquid and browning sauce into flour paste. Cook in oven 2 minutes. Stir well with wire whisk; cook in oven 2 minutes, stir after 1 minute. Add cubed lamb and remaining ingredients, mix well. Cover, cook in oven 5 minutes. Place cooked pie crust on top of stew mixture. Cook in oven 2 minutes, turning 180° after 1 minute. Makes 6 servings.

Conventional Cooking:
1. *Prepare stew ingredients as directed. Turn into casserole. Cook in a moderate oven about 1 hour. Cover with prepared crust.*
2. *Bake in moderate oven, 375°, 12 minutes until crust is brown.*

DUBLIN LAMB STEW

4 tablespoons vegetable oil, divided

2½ pounds boneless lamb, cut in chunks

Seasoned flour (salt and pepper)

1 medium onion, chopped

½ cup sliced celery

½ teaspoon poultry seasoning

1 teaspoon sugar

Salt and pepper

2 cups boiling water

6 carrots, cut in ½-inch chunks

8 small onions, peeled

4 medium potatoes, pared and quartered

1 package (10 oz.) frozen green peas, partially thawed and broken apart

Heat large Browning Skillet in Radarange oven 4½ minutes. Add half the oil, and lamb chunks rolled in seasoned flour. Cook in oven 1½ minutes; turn meat over, cook 1½ minutes more. Put browned lamb in 4-quart covered casserole. Wipe skillet out with paper towels. Heat skillet in oven 2½ minutes. Add remaining oil and lamb chunks, and cook as before; add to casserole with browned lamb. Cook chopped onion, celery, and seasonings in Browning Skillet 2 minutes, stir once. Add to casserole with lamb, add boiling water, carrots and potatoes. Cover, cook in oven 15 minutes, stirring after 7½ minutes cooking. Add partially thawed peas, cook 7½ minutes more. Let stand 10 minutes before serving. Gravy may be thickened with flour or cornstarch, if desired. Add color with a teaspoon of browning sauce if desired. Makes 6 servings.

Conventional Cooking:
1. Brown lamb, combine remaining ingredients in Dutch oven.
2. Cover, cook over medium heat for 1½ to 2 hours.

FRUITED MEAT LOAF

2½ pounds lean ground beef	2 teaspoons salt
1½ cups packaged stuffing mix	⅛ teaspoon pepper
2 cups finely chopped apples	2 tablespoons prepared mustard
½ cup chopped onion	2 tablespoons prepared horseradish
3 eggs	¾ cup catchup

Thoroughly mix together all ingredients. Pack into an 8-inch-square baking dish. Cook in Radarange oven uncovered 20 minutes, turning the dish one quarter turn every 5 minutes. Let stand a few minutes before serving. Makes 8 to 10 servings.

Conventional Cooking:
1. Mix together all ingredients as directed. Pack into greased loaf pan.
2. Bake in moderate oven, 350°, about 1 hour or until done.

FRUITED PORK ROAST

1 can (8¼ oz.) sliced
   pineapple
1 cup spiced crab apples
⅓ cup brown sugar

½ teaspoon allspice
¼ cup wine vinegar
1 pork loin (4½–5 pounds)

Drain ⅓ cup juice from fruits into 2-cup glass measure or bowl. Reserve fruit. Mix in sugar, vinegar, and spice. Cook in Radarange oven 5 minutes; stir once. Place pork, fat side down, in 2-quart baking dish. Cook in oven 10 minutes. Baste roast with warm fruit sauce; turn dish around 180° in oven. Cook 10 minutes more. Turn roast fat side up, baste. Cook 10 minutes more. Check internal temperature with meat thermometer. Pork is done at 170°. If roast is not done, remove thermometer, and cook 5 to 10 minutes more. Insert thermometer, cover roast, let stand 10 minutes till thermometer registers 170°. Garnish roast with reserved fruit. (Refrigerate unused juice mixture for later use as ham or pork baste.) Makes 6 to 8 servings.

Conventional Cooking:
1. *Place pork in roasting pan fat side up, baste with warm fruit sauce.*
2. *Roast uncovered, at 325°, basting occasionally, allowing 30 to 35 minutes per pound. Serve as above.*

GERMAN FRESH HAM AND SAUERKRAUT

2 pounds fresh ham steak
¼ cup seasoned flour (salt and pepper)
1 tablespoon oil
1 large onion, chopped
2 celery tops, chopped
2 cups hot water or stock

2 tablespoons cider vinegar
1 can (1 lb.) sauerkraut
3 tablespoons brown sugar
1 teaspoon caraway seeds
1 teaspoon salt
1 tart apple, diced

Cut ham into 4 pieces, slash on edge to keep it from curling; rub well with seasoned flour. Preheat large Browning Skillet in Radarange oven 4½ minutes, add oil and floured meat. Cook in oven uncovered 4 minutes, turning pieces over after 2 minutes. Add onion, celery, water, and vinegar; cover, cook in oven 8 minutes. Spread sauerkraut in layer on top of meat, sprinkle with brown sugar, caraway seeds, salt and apple. Cover, cook 8 minutes more. Let stand a few minutes before serving. Makes 4 servings.

Conventional Cooking:
1. Sear pork in heavy fry pan or Dutch oven. Add next 5 ingredients. Cover, cook on top of stove about 1 hour. Add sauerkraut and remaining ingredients.
2. Cover, cook on top of stove over low heat 45 to 50 minutes.

GLAZED SMOKED PORK BUTT

1 boneless smoked pork butt (about 2½ pounds)
18 whole cloves

½ cup firmly packed brown sugar
¼ cup prepared mustard

Place pork butt in deep casserole, add boiling water to just cover. Cover, cook in Radarange oven 20 minutes, until fork tender. Turn meat over in liquid, turn dish 180° at end of 10 minutes. Take meat from broth, place in shallow baking dish. Stud meat all over with cloves. Mix sugar and mustard to a smooth paste, spread half over top of meat. Cook in oven, uncovered, 7½ minutes. Turn meat over, add remaining sauce to top of meat, cook in oven 5 to 7½ minutes more. Remove meat from oven, insert meat thermometer and cover with foil to keep warm. Let stand until meat thermometer reaches 170° internal temperature. Makes 6 to 8 servings.

Conventional Cooking:
1. *Place meat on rack in shallow pan.*
2. *Bake in slow oven (325°) 45 minutes per pound. Add glaze last half hour.*

GOURMET BEEF STEW

¾-pound beef stew meat
1 tablespoon flour
½ teaspoon salt
1 tablespoon shortening or other fat
1 can (6 oz.) tomato sauce
Clove of garlic, minced
Dash powdered bay leaf
Dash thyme
½ teaspoon monosodium glutamate

¾ cup consomme, water, or dry red wine
2 teaspoons vinegar
2 carrots, peeled and sliced (¾ cup)
1 medium potato, diced (¾ cup)
1 stalk celery, sliced
6 small whole onions
½ cup frozen green peas

Cut beef in 2-inch pieces. Coat meat with flour and salt which have been combined. Preheat large Browning Skillet in Radarange oven 4½ minutes, add floured beef cubes and shortening. Cook 1½ minutes, stir; cook 1½ minutes more. Add tomato sauce, seasonings, consomme or other liquid, and vinegar. Cover, and cook in Radarange oven for 20 minutes, or until beef is tender. Arrange carrots, potato, celery, and onions in skillet. Cover and cook 9 to 10 minutes longer or until vegetables are just tender. Sprinkle frozen peas over stew and cook 1 minute longer. Correct seasoning before serving. Makes 4 servings.

Conventional Cooking:
1. *Brown meat as directed, add seasonings and liquid ingredients, cover, and cook till meat is tender.*
2. *Add remaining ingredients, cover, and cook on low until vegetables are barely tender, about 30 minutes more.*

HAMBURG "NESTS"

2 tablespoons butter or
    margarine
¼ cup onion, chopped
½ green pepper, chopped
1 pound ground beef
2 cups soft white bread
    crumbs
Salt and pepper

1 tablespoon prepared
    mustard
Milk
Cereal crumbs (about ¼
    cup)
4 small eggs
¼ cup shredded Swiss
    cheese

Preheat small Browning Skillet in Radarange oven 2½ minutes. Place butter, onion, and green pepper in small Browning Skillet; cook in oven 1 minute, stir once. Mix with beef, bread crumbs, and seasonings. Form meat mixture into 4 doughnut-shaped rings, about 4″ in diameter. Brush with a little milk; coat with cereal crumbs. Chill (rings will hold shape and be easier to handle if cold, but this is optional). Arrange meat nests in a greased shallow baking dish. Cook in oven 2 minutes. Turn dish around 180°, cook 2 minutes more. Break an egg into each "nest" (remember to pierce yolk); top with cheese. Cook in oven 3 to 4 minutes, or to desired doneness for eggs. Let stand 2 to 3 minutes. Serve with shredded lettuce and pickle garnish. Makes 4 servings.

Conventional Cooking:
1. *Arrange meat "doughnuts" in a greased baking dish. Cook in moderate oven, 350°, 15 to 20 minutes.*
2. *Break an egg into each ring, top with cheese. Cook at 350° for 5 minutes, or to desired doneness.*

HASH STUFFED SQUASH

2 medium size acorn squash
   (about 2 pounds)
4 slices of bacon, halved
Salt
4 teaspoons brown sugar,
   divided

1 can (1 lb.) roast beef
   hash
⅓ cup catchup

Pierce acorn squash several times with the blade of a knife. Cook squash whole on paper towels in Radarange oven 5 minutes. Remove squash. Cook bacon between layers of paper towels 2 minutes. Cut squash in half, scoop out seeds; place squash in shallow baking dish. Salt cavities, sprinkle with brown sugar. Cover; cook in oven 4 minutes. Pack hash into squash hollows, mounding if necessary. Coat with catchup. Top each squash with 2 half-slices partially cooked bacon. Cook in oven 8 to 10 minutes until squash is tender and bacon cooked. Makes 4 servings.

Conventional Cooking:

1. *Place squash cut side down in shallow baking pan, add ½ cup water. Bake in moderate oven, 350°, about 20 minutes. Drain squash, sprinkle cavities with salt and sugar. Fill with hash, coat with catchup.*
2. *Return squash to oven, bake 30 to 35 minutes. Top with bacon last 10 minutes of baking.*

LITTLE MEAT LOAVES

1 egg
¾ cup evaporated milk
1 cup soft white bread
  crumbs
1½ teaspoons salt
¼ teaspoon seasoned
  pepper

½ teaspoon Italian seasoning or poultry seasoning
1 tablespoon instant minced
  onion
1½ pounds ground beef

Glaze:

⅓ cup orange marmalade
1 teaspoon vinegar

½ teaspoon bottled brown-
  ing sauce

Mix together well all meat loaf ingredients. Shape mix into 4 individual loaves. Place loaves in shallow 2-quart baking dish. Cook in Radarange oven 10 minutes, turning dish 180° at 3 minute intervals. Carefully turn loaves over halfway through cooking time. Mix together glaze ingredients, brush or spoon over tops and sides of meat loaves. Cook in oven 2 minutes, turning dish twice. Let stand 5 minutes. Makes 4 individual loaves or servings.

Conventional Cooking:
1. Mix and shape loaves as directed. Place in shallow baking pan.
2. Bake in a moderate oven, 350°, about 35 minutes. Baste with glaze during last 10 minutes of cooking.

LIVER DE LUXE

2 pounds beef or lamb liver, sliced
Salt, pepper, and flour
1 large sweet onion, thinly sliced and separated into rings
1 cup packaged stuffing mix, crushed

1 can (4 oz.) chopped mushrooms, drained
½ cup chopped raw bacon (3 slices)
2 tablespoons minced parsley
½ cup beef broth

Arrange liver slices in 2-quart oblong glass baking dish. Sprinkle with salt, pepper, and a little flour. Cover with a layer of onion rings. Mix together next 4 ingredients; sprinkle over onion. Add broth. Cover, and cook in Radarange oven 21 to 22 minutes, turning dish halfway around every 7 minutes. Let stand covered 10 minutes before serving. Makes 8 servings.

Conventional Cooking:
1. *Arrange liver as directed.*
2. *Bake, covered, in 350° oven about 45 minutes. (Additional beef broth may be needed; ¼ to ½ cup.)*

LONDON BROIL

1 flank steak (1–1½ pounds)
1 tablespoon sugar
2 tablespoons soy sauce
2 tablespoons sherry
1 clove garlic, minced

1 tablespoon honey
1 teaspoon salt
⅛ teaspoon pepper
2 tablespoons vegetable oil, divided

Pierce steak all over with a sharp fork. Mix together remaining ingredients (except oil); pour over steak. Let stand covered in the refrigerator 10 to 12 hours, turning occasionally. Remove from refrigerator one hour before cooking. Heat large Browning Skillet in Radarange oven 4½ minutes.

Cut steak in two pieces to fit skillet. Pat dry with paper towel. Add 1 tablespoon oil, and steak, cook in oven 2 minutes per side for well done.* To cook remaining half of steak: wipe skillet with paper towel, heat in oven 2 minutes. Add oil and steak. Cook to desired degree of doneness. To serve, slice meat into very thin slices, carving at an angle, against the grain. Makes 4 to 6 servings.

*Cook one minute per side for rare, 1½ minutes per side for medium.

Conventional Cooking:
1. *Prepare as above.*
2. *Cook steak under broiler to desired degree of doneness. Rare—4 to 5 minutes per side. Medium—6 minutes per side. Well done—8 minutes per side.*

NEW ENGLAND POT ROAST

2 cups buttermilk	2 bay leaves
2 teaspoons seasoned salt	Few whole allspice
½ teaspoon pepper	4 pounds bottom round
1 garlic clove, mashed	roast

Mix buttermilk with seasonings to make a marinade. Place meat in large bowl, add marinade. Cover; refrigerate overnight, turning roast several times. Drain meat; pat dry with paper towels. Place meat in large covered casserole. Cook in Radarange oven 15 minutes, turn roast over, cook 10 to 15 minutes more. Remove from oven, insert meat thermometer after 30 minutes cooking time. Check doneness, cook 5 minutes more if more well-done roast is desired. Makes 8 to 10 servings.

Conventional Cooking:
1. *Prepare roast in marinade as directed. Brown roast in 2 tablespoons vegetable oil in a Dutch oven. Add about 1 cup of reserved marinade.*
2. *Cook, covered tightly, over low heat for 4 hours.*

91

ORANGE GLAZED PORK ROAST

½ cup orange marmalade
2 tablespoons vinegar

3–4 pound boned and rolled
pork roast

Mix marmalade and vinegar; heat in Radarange oven 1 minute. Cut 4-inch wide strips of foil wrap. Wrap around the ends of the roast, patting all edges smooth.* Place pork roast on rack in 2-quart oblong pan. Cook in oven 7 to 10 minutes depending on size of pork roast.† Remove foil covers from roast ends. Brush top with orange glaze. Turn dish 180°. Cook in oven 7 to 10 more minutes. Turn roast over; baste; cook 7 to 10 minutes. Check internal temperature of roast with meat thermometer. Pork is done at 170° internal temperature. If more time is needed, turn dish 180° and baste roast. Cook 7 to 10 minutes more. Remove from oven; insert meat thermometer, cover with foil. Let stand 10 minutes or until meat thermometer reaches 170°. Makes 5 to 6 servings.

*The foil acts as a shield to keep the ends of the pork roast from overcooking.

†Pork is cooked 10 minutes per pound. A deboned rolled roast may cook faster than a bone-in roast.

Conventional Cooking:
1. *Mix and heat marmalade and vinegar to make baste. Prepare roast as directed. Roast in moderate oven, 325°, 1 hour.*
2. *Apply baste and continue roasting for about 1 hour, brushing with baste every 10 minutes, or until it is used up.*

PORK CHOPS HAWAII

4 pork chops, cut 1-inch
    thick (about 1½ pounds)
2 tablespoons soy sauce
2 tablespoons vegetable oil
Salt and pepper
4 slices canned pineapple

4 large tender prunes, pitted
¼ cup chunky peanut
    butter
8 medium size carrots,
    scraped
½ cup water or broth

Heat Browning Skillet in Radarange oven 4½ minutes. Brush chops with soy sauce. Add oil and chops to skillet. Cook uncovered in Radarange oven 5 minutes, turning chops after 2½ minutes. Place a slice of pineapple and a prune stuffed with peanut butter on each chop. Arrange carrots around chops; add water. Cover, cook in oven about 12 minutes, until fork tender. Turn skillet 180° after 6 minutes. Let stand 10 minutes before serving. Makes 4 servings.

Conventional Cooking:
1. *Brown chops in hot oil, remove to a baking dish. Prepare as directed with remaining ingredients.*
2. *Cover, bake in a moderate oven, 350°, about 1 hour. Remove cover during last 10 minutes of cooking.*

PORK CHOPS MAUI

4 center cut pork chops,
    cut 1-inch thick
1 garlic clove
1 teaspoon salt
¼ teaspoon seasoned
    pepper
Dash Tabasco sauce
½ teaspoon ground ginger

½ teaspoon grated orange
    peel
¼ cup brown sugar
3 tablespoons cider vinegar
½ cup canned, crushed
    pineapple, drained
1 small white onion, cut up

Heat Browning Skillet in Radarange oven 4½ minutes. Add chops, cook in oven 5 minutes, turning once. Drain off fat. Mix together remaining ingredients in blender; process until smooth. Pour over chops. Cover, cook in oven 3½ minutes, turn dish halfway around and cook another 3½ to 4 minutes. Let stand 5 minutes before serving. Makes 4 servings.

Conventional Cooking:
1. Place chops in shallow baking dish. Cook, covered, in moderate oven about 25 minutes, turning once.
2. Add sauce, cover. Bake in oven about 40 minutes, until very tender.

QUICK CASSOULET

½ pound small sausage links, cut in half

1 cup chopped onion

1 clove garlic, minced

1½ cups boiling water

1 tablespoon minced parsley

½ teaspoon leaf thyme, crushed

2 cups cooked cubed lamb*

2 jars (1 lb. ea.) Boston-style baked beans

1 can (8 oz.) tomato sauce

¼ cup toasted Buttered Bread Crumbs (page 223)

Heat large Browning Skillet in Radarange oven 4½ minutes. Add sausage, onion, and garlic. Cook uncovered in oven 3 minutes, stirring once. Add water and seasonings, and lamb; cover, cook in oven 3 minutes. Drain off liquid and reserve. Spread a layer of beans in a 3-quart earthenware or glass casserole. Add a layer of drained sausage, lamb, and onion. Cover with a layer of baked beans. Mix tomato sauce into liquid in which meat was cooked; pour over beans in casserole. Top with crumbs. Cover, cook in oven 12 minutes, turning casserole 180° at 6 minutes. Makes 6 servings.

*Or other cooked meat or poultry.

Conventional Cooking:

1. Combine as directed above after browning sausage, onion, and garlic with 2 tablespoons vegetable oil.
2. Layer in casserole dish and bake 75 minutes covered in 325° oven. Remove cover for last 10 minutes.

RAGOUT BRITTANY

1½ pounds top or bottom round steak
Seasoned flour (salt and pepper)
2–3 tablespoons vegetable oil, divided
1 teaspoon instant coffee
1 beef bouillon cube, crushed
1 cup boiling water
1 can (8 oz.) tomato sauce
1 teaspoon salt
¼ teaspoon pepper

½ teaspoon crumbled oregano
Pinch cloves
1 bay leaf
4 medium potatoes, pared (1 lb.)
2 large onions, quartered
1 cup red wine (Burgundy)
1 can (8 oz.) tiny carrots, drained
1 package (10 oz.) frozen cut green beans, partially thawed

Preheat large Browning Skillet in Radarange oven 4½ minutes. Cut meat in 1-inch cubes, roll in seasoned flour. Add half oil and meat to skillet, cook in oven 3 minutes, stirring after 1½ minutes. Add browned meat to large 3½-to 4-quart covered casserole. Wipe excess grease out of Browning Skillet with paper towel. Heat skillet 2½ minutes in oven, add remaining oil and meat. Cook as before. Add to large casserole. Mix the next 9 ingredients, pour over meat. Cut potatoes in ½-inch slices, roll in remaining flour. Add potatoes and onions to casserole. Cook 8 minutes, covered, stir well, cook 8 minutes more. Add wine, carrots, and green beans. Stir well, cover, and cook 15 minutes longer, stirring halfway through cooking. Remove from oven, let stand covered 10 minutes. Thicken gravy if desired before serving. Makes 6 servings.

Conventional Cooking:
1. *Prepare meat and brown in hot oil in Dutch oven. Add liquids and seasonings, adding 1 extra cup water. Cover, cook over medium heat 1 hour.*
2. *Add potatoes, onions, and carrots, cover. Simmer about 40 minutes. Add beans and wine. Simmer about 15 minutes.*

RUSSIAN LAMB

2 pounds boned lamb
   shoulder
Grated peel 1 lemon
Juice 2 lemons
½ cup minced parsley
1 teaspoon dried dill weed

¼ teaspoon ground garlic
1 teaspoon salt
½ teaspoon black pepper
3 tablespoons vegetable oil,
   divided

Cut lamb in 1½-inch cubes. Place in a deep bowl. Mix together lemon peel, lemon juice, parsley, seasonings, and 1 tablespoon oil, pour over lamb. Refrigerate 4 to 5 hours; drain. Let stand at room temperature 45 minutes to an hour before cooking. Heat Browning Skillet in Radarange oven 4½ minutes. Add remaining 2 tablespoons oil, and lamb. Cook in oven 2 minutes, turning meat to brown on all sides. Cover, cook in oven 14 to 15 minutes, stirring three times. Serve over cooked kasha, or brown rice. If desired, stir 1 to 2 tablespoons flour into juice remaining in skillet to make a paste. Stir until smooth. Cook in oven 1½ minutes, stirring twice; pour over meat. Makes 4 servings.

Conventional Cooking:
1. *Marinate lamb cubes as directed. Drain. Sauté cubes in hot oil to brown on all sides. Cover.*
2. *Cook over medium heat about 25 minutes until tender.*

96

SAUERBRATEN

3 pounds sirloin tip
1½ cups red wine vinegar
1½ cups water
1 large onion, sliced
½ lemon, sliced
2 tablespoons mixed
  pickling spice
1½ teaspoons salt

2 tablespoons sugar
Flour
1 tablespoon vegetable oil
¼ cup butter or margarine
¼ cup flour
2 teaspoons light brown
  sugar
10 gingersnaps, crushed

Place meat in deep bowl. Mix together vinegar, water, and next 5 ingredients; pour over meat. Cover and refrigerate for 48 hours, turning meat in liquid twice a day. Take meat from refrigerator 1 hour before cooking. Drain meat, reserve liquid. Pat meat dry with paper towels, and rub meat lightly with flour. Heat large Browning Skillet in Radarange oven 4½ minutes. Add oil and meat, cook in oven 1 minute per side. Remove meat to a 2- to 2½-quart covered casserole. Cook in oven on defrost or slow-cook cycle 30 minutes. Turn meat over, add 1 cup reserve strained marinade. Continue cooking on defrost for 15 minutes more.

In another bowl or glass measure melt the butter 30 seconds. Stir in flour and brown sugar to make a smooth paste. Add 1 cup more strained marinade, stirring constantly. Cook in oven 2 minutes, stirring every 30 seconds. Remove meat to a warm serving platter. Stir sauce mixture into liquid in casserole. Cook in oven 3 minutes, stir once. Add crushed gingersnaps, cook in oven 1 minute, stir smooth. Serve with sliced meat. Makes 6 to 8 servings.

Conventional Cooking:
1. Marinate meat as directed. Reserve marinade. Brown meat on both sides, add 1 cup of marinade, cover and cook over low heat about 3 hours or until tender.
2. For gravy: melt butter, stir in flour and sugar to make a smooth paste. Add 1 cup reserved marinade and cooking juices from meat. Cook, stirring, until thick. Add crushed gingersnaps and cook a few minutes more.

SAVORY LAMB SHANKS

4 lamb shanks (about 1
    pound each), approx-
    imately 4 pounds, divided
2 garlic cloves, split in half
2 tablespoons vegetable oil,
    divided

1½ cups boiling water
1 packet onion soup mix
1 can (8 oz.) tomato sauce
1 teaspoon Worcestershire
    sauce

Wipe lamb shanks with a damp cloth. Cut a slit in each shank, insert a half of garlic clove in each slit. Preheat large Browning Skillet in Radarange oven 4½ minutes; add half the oil and 2 lamb shanks. Cook in oven 45 seconds per side, turning once. Remove shanks to a 4-quart covered casserole. Wipe excess grease out of Browning Skillet with paper towels. Heat skillet in oven 2½ minutes. Add rest of oil and lamb shanks, cooking as above; add browned shanks to casserole, and all remaining ingredients. Cover, cook 15 minutes. Turn lamb shanks over, cook on defrost or slow-cook cycle 30 minutes. Turn lamb shanks over again, cook 10 to 15 minutes more on defrost cycle till meat is fork tender. Let stand covered a few minutes before serving. Makes 4 servings.

Conventional Cooking:
1. *Prepare shanks with garlic. Brown in hot oil in heavy fry pan or Dutch oven. Add remaining ingredients. Cover.*
2. *Cook in moderate oven, 375°, about 1½ to 2 hours, or until tender.*

SAVORY MEAT LOAF

½ pound ground pork
1 cup catchup, divided
1½ pounds ground beef
2 cups soft bread crumbs
1 green pepper, chopped
2 medium eggs, beaten
2 teaspoons salt

1 teaspoon ground celery
  seed
⅛ teaspoon seasoned
  pepper
1 tablespoon mustard
1 teaspoon Worcestershire
  sauce

Cook ground pork on plastic cooking rack in 2-quart utility dish in the Radarange oven 3 minutes, drain. Combine pork with ¾ cup catchup and all remaining ingredients; mix thoroughly; shape into round loaf. Place in 9-inch pie plate. Spread surface with remaining ¼ cup catchup. Cook in oven 15 minutes, turning the dish ¼ turn every 3 minutes. Let stand 8 minutes before serving. Serve cut in pie-shape wedges. Makes 8 servings.

Conventional Cooking:
1. Cook ground pork, drain. Mix meat loaf as directed above.
2. Bake at 350° about 1 hour.

SPANISH BEEF ROLL

3 slices bacon, diced
1½ pounds round steak, cut
  ½-inch thick
1 tablespoon flour
2 hard-cooked eggs,
  chopped
⅓ cup chopped stuffed
  olives
1 small onion, chopped

1 tablespoon capers,
  chopped
½ teaspoon salt
¼ teaspoon pepper
2 teaspoons bottled browning sauce, plus 1 tablespoon water
1 cup beef broth

Cook diced bacon between layers of paper towels in the Radarange oven 2½ minutes. Let cool. Rub meat with flour on side placed up; pound with the edge of a heavy plate to

99

thin slightly. Mix together bacon and next 6 ingredients; spread on meat. Roll up from wide end; tie with strings. Brush half browning sauce and water mixture over top of roll. Place in 1½-quart oblong casserole in the oven, add beef broth; cover with plastic film wrap. Cook 7 minutes; turn dish 180°. Cook 10 minutes on defrost or slow-cook cycle. Turn over, brush with remaining browning sauce, cook 10 minutes on defrost. Let stand 5 to 10 minutes before carving. Thicken sauce if desired with 2 tablespoons cornstarch stirred into hot sauce with a wire whisk till lumps are removed; then cook in oven 2 to 2½ minutes. stirring several times. Serve over meat slices. Makes 4 servings.

Conventional Cooking:
1. *Prepare beef roll as directed above. omitting browning sauce. Brown in large skillet over medium heat. Place beef roll in oven-proof casserole, add beef broth.*
2. *Cover and cook at 350° for 1 hour.*

SPANISH LAMB CHOPS

1 tablespoon vegetable oil
4 shoulder lamb chops
(about 2 pounds)
½ cup chopped onion
1 small green pepper, sliced
1 can (1 lb.) stewed
tomatoes

4 slices lemon
Salt to taste
1 cup finely chopped cooked
ham

Heat large Browning Skillet in Radarange oven 4½ minutes. Add oil and chops, cook in oven 2 minutes; turn chops, cook 2 minutes more. Add onion, green pepper, tomatoes, lemon, and salt. Cover, cook on defrost setting 30 minutes; turn dish around 180° after 15 minutes of cooking and add the ham. Makes 4 servings.

Conventional Cooking:
1. *Brown chops in oil on medium high heat. Transfer to casserole, and add remaining ingredients.*
2. *Bake covered at 350° for 1 hour.*

SPICED CIDER BAKED HAM

2 center cut slices ready-to-
   eat ham, cut 1-inch thick
Whole cloves
1 large onion, sliced

3 tablespoons brown sugar
1 cup sweet cider or apple
   juice

Score ham fat, stud with cloves. Heat large Browning Skillet in Radarange oven 4½ minutes. Add one ham steak; cook 45 seconds per side. Remove ham steak, heat skillet 2 minutes, add second ham steak; cook 45 seconds per side. Return first steak to skillet. Add onion, sugar, and cider. Cover; cook in oven 6 to 8 minutes, turning skillet a complete turn halfway through cooking time. Makes 4 servings.

Sauce:

½ cup corn syrup
½ cup seedless raisins
¼ teaspoon cinnamon

⅛ teaspoon nutmeg
2 tablespoons cornstarch
2 tablespoons water

Drain liquid from ham, measure ½ cup into a small bowl. Mix in corn syrup and raisins; cook in oven 45 seconds. Stir in spices and cornstarch blended with 2 tablespoons water. Cook in Radarange oven 2 minutes until thickened. Stir twice during cooking time. Serve sauce with ham.

Conventional Cooking:
1. Brown ham in small amount of fat in large skillet over medium heat, about 12 minutes.
2. Add remaining ingredients, bake in 350° oven for 1 hour.

STEAK BIRDS

1 cup brown rice
2 pounds round steak, cut
   ½-inch thick
1 tablespoon flour
½ teaspoon garlic powder
3 tablespoons packaged
   seasoned bread crumbs
2 tablespoons instant onion
2 tablespoons instant
   minced parsley

2 tablespoons grated Parmesan cheese
½ teaspoon salt
2 tablespoons oil
½ cup red wine
½ cup water
¼ cup catchup
1–2 tablespoons flour
¼ cup liquid

Cook brown rice according to package directions to yield 1 cup. Rub meat with flour and garlic powder. Pound meat until about ¼ inch thick; cut into 4 pieces. Mix next 6 ingredients to make a stuffing. If mixture is too crumbly, add 2 to 3 tablespoons wine or water to moisten. Spread equal amounts stuffing over the 4 meat pieces; roll up, secure with wooden picks or tie with string. Heat large Browning Skillet in Radarange oven 4½ minutes. Add oil and meat rolls. Cook in oven 4 minutes, turning meat rolls at 2 minutes to brown all sides. Mix together wine, water, and catchup; pour over meat. Cover, cook in oven 6 minutes, turning skillet 180° after 6 minutes. Mix 1 to 2 tablespoons flour with ¼ cup water, broth, or wine. Stir into liquid in skillet. Cook in oven 2 minutes, stirring several times. Cover, let stand 8 to 10 minutes before serving. Serve meat rolls with pan gravy. Makes 4 servings.

Conventional Cooking:
1. Sear meat rolls on all sides in hot fry pan. Place in shallow casserole, add liquid, and cover.
2. Bake in moderate oven, 350°, about 2 hours until meat is very tender and succulent.

STEAK PALERMO

2 pounds sirloin steak (cut ¾–1-inch thick) cut in 2 pieces
1 cup herb-seasoned bread stuffing mix, crushed
1 teaspoon coarse ground black pepper
1 teaspoon salt
½ teaspoon garlic powder
½ teaspoon rosemary
½ teaspoon basil
2 tablespoons Italian style salad dressing
2 tablespoons soft butter

Wipe steak with paper towels. Place on cutting board, pierce all over using a two-tined kitchen fork. Thoroughly mix remaining ingredients. Spread steak with ½ the crumb mixture. Press the crumbs into the steak, using the bottom of a heavy cup or mug. Turn steak over and repeat with remaining crumbs. Place in shallow baking dish. Cover with plastic film. Makes 6 servings.

To cook:
Rare (Pink)—Cook in Radarange oven 3 minutes; turn dish 180°, cook 2 to 3 minutes more. Let stand few minutes before slicing.
Medium—Cook in Radarange oven 4 minutes; turn dish 180°, cook 3 to 4 minutes more. Let stand a few minutes before slicing.
Well Done—Cook in Radarange oven 5 minutes; turn dish 180°, cook 4 to 5 minutes more. Let stand a few minutes before slicing.
To slice meat: use a sharp knife to slice very thin across the grain.

Conventional Cooking:
1. Arrange crumbed steak in a shallow casserole.
2. Bake uncovered for 30 minutes at 450°.

STEAK WITH ONIONS

1½ pounds boneless round
   steak (cut ¾-inch thick)
Meat tenderizer
2 tablespoons oil, divided
2 large mild onions, sliced

1 teaspoon salt
½ teaspoon pepper
1 cup beef broth
2 tablespoons butter or
   margarine

Trim fat from steak, cut in 2 pieces, slash edges to prevent curling. Prepare steak with tenderizer as directed on package. Preheat large Browning Skillet in Radarange oven 4½ minutes. Add oil and half the steak. Cook 1 minute per side. Remove to 2-quart oblong dish, cover. Wipe skillet out with paper towels. Heat 2½ minutes, add oil and other steak half. Cook 1 minute per side. Add to cooked steak in casserole. Spread onions over meat; sprinkle with salt and pepper, add broth, dot with butter. Cover with plastic film wrap; cook in oven 8 minutes. Turn dish around 180°; cook on defrost or slow-cook cycle 10 minutes; turn dish 180°, cook on defrost setting 10 minutes more. Makes 4 servings.

Conventional Cooking:
1. Heat heavy fry pan. Add oil and steak, sear quickly on both sides. Spread onions, seasonings, and butter over meat. Add broth. Cover.
2. Cook over low medium heat about 60 minutes.

STUFFED LAMB ROAST

3 to 4 pound shoulder lamb
   roast
½ teaspoon seasoned
   pepper
¼ teaspoon powdered
   garlic
¼ teaspoon crushed
   rosemary

2 cups packaged herb
   stuffing mix
2 tablespoons minced onion
¼ cup minced celery
⅓ cup soft butter or
   margarine
1 cup red wine, divided
Flour

Have bones removed from meat. Flatten meat; sprinkle with combined seasonings on both sides. Use back of spoon to press and rub seasonings into meat. Mix together stuffing mix, onion, celery, butter, and ½ cup of the wine; spread on meat (or make a pocket in meat and fill with stuffing). Roll and tie meat. Dust with flour; place in 3- to 4-quart casserole, fat side down. Cook covered 10 minutes in Radarange oven; turn dish 180°, cook 10 minutes more. Turn roast over, add wine, cover, cook 10 minutes; turn dish 180°, cover, cook 6 to 10 minutes more. Let stand a few minutes, covered, with a meat thermometer inserted in thickest part of roast. Temperature should reach 180°. Makes 6 servings.

Conventional Cooking:
1. *Place prepared roast in shallow pan in preheated moderate oven, 325°.*
2. *Roast about 1 hour 40 minutes. Baste with remaining wine during last 20 minutes of cooking.*

TANGY BROWN RIBS

2 *pounds meaty pork spareribs*	2 *tablespoons brown sugar*
Pepper	1 *teaspoon prepared mustard*
1 *onion, finely chopped*	*Dash Tabasco sauce*
2 *tablespoons vinegar*	1 *can (15 oz.) tomato sauce with tomato bits*
1 *teaspoon salt*	

Place ribs in 2-quart baking dish, sprinkle with pepper. Cook in Radarange oven 10 minutes. Drain off fat; turn ribs. Cook in oven 15 minutes. Mix together onions, vinegar, salt, sugar, mustard, and Tabasco; spread on ribs. Pour tomato sauce over all. Cook in oven 5 minutes. Turn ribs, spoon sauce over, cook in oven 5 minutes. Makes 4 servings.

Conventional Cooking:
1. *Make sauce for ribs, baste.*
2. *Cook ribs in hot oven, 400°, for about 40 minutes. Turn several times and drain off fat once or twice.*

UPSIDE-DOWN MEAT LOAF

¾ cup packaged bread
   stuffing mix
½ cup milk
⅓ cup catchup
1 onion, chopped
1½ pounds lean ground
   beef
¼ teaspoon basil

½ teaspoon salt
⅛ teaspoon seasoned
   pepper
Dash Tabasco sauce
½ teaspoon Worcestershire
   sauce
4 canned peach halves

Measure stuffing mix into a bowl, add milk and catchup; let stand 15 minutes. Add remaining ingredients (except peaches); mix thoroughly. Arrange peach halves, cut side down, in sprayed 8″x5″x3″ loaf pan; cover with meat mixture. Cook uncovered in Radarange oven 15 minutes, turning dish 180° halfway through cooking time. Drain off liquid; let stand 5 minutes. Unmold on serving platter; fill center of peach halves with cranberry sauce or currant jelly. Makes 6 servings.

Conventional Cooking:
1. Prepare meat loaf as directed, placing peach halves in bottom of loaf dish.
2. Bake meat loaf in 350° oven for 1 hour.

VEAL SCALOPPINE MILANO

1 tablespoon olive oil
1 garlic clove, crushed
1 pound thinly sliced veal
   cutlet, cut into 4 servings
¾ cup sliced onion
1 can (4 oz.) mushrooms,
   drained

2 tablespoons flour
½ teaspoon salt
⅛ teaspoon pepper
Dash thyme
1 can (8 oz.) tomato sauce
½ cup beef broth

Heat large Browning Skillet in Radarange oven 4½ minutes. Add oil, garlic, and veal. Cook in oven 2 minutes, turning veal after 1 minute. Remove veal and reserve. Discard garlic. Add onion and mushrooms to skillet; cook in oven 3 minutes. Stir in flour, salt, pepper, and thyme; cook in oven 30 seconds. Gradually stir in tomato sauce and water. Cook in oven 2 minutes; stir once. Return veal to skillet, pushing it down into sauce and spooning sauce over. Cook in oven 5 to 6 minutes, or until veal is tender. Makes 4 servings.

Conventional Cooking:
1. *Sauté veal pieces in hot oil with garlic. Sauté mushrooms and onion in same oil. Combine remaining ingredients to make a sauce; pour over veal and vegetables.*
2. *Cover, cook over medium heat until veal is tender, 35 to 40 minutes.*

VEAL STEAK WITH DUMPLINGS

2 tablespoons vegetable oil, divided
2 pounds veal steak cut into 2-inch pieces, divided
Seasoned flour
1 teaspoon paprika

¼ teaspoon pepper
1 cup hot water or broth
1 can (10½ oz.) condensed cream of chicken soup
1 can (1 lb.) small white onions

Heat large Browning Skillet in Radarange oven 4½ minutes. Add 1 tablespoon oil and half the veal pieces dredged in seasoned flour. Cook in oven 2 minutes, stirring once to brown on all sides. Remove meat from skillet to a 2½-quart casserole. Wipe skillet with paper toweling, heat again 2 minutes, and add oil and rest of floured veal pieces. Cook 2 minutes, stirring once. Transfer to casserole with rest of meat. Mix remaining ingredients; add to meat. Cover, cook in oven 5 minutes. Stir, top with dumplings. Cook uncovered in oven 5 minutes. Cover and let stand 5 minutes before serving. Makes 6 to 8 servings.

Dumplings:

1 cup all purpose flour
2 teaspoons baking powder
¼ teaspoon salt
½ teaspoon poultry
  seasoning
½ teaspoon instant minced
  onion
¼ teaspoon crushed celery
  seed

2 tablespoons vegetable oil
½ cup milk
¼ cup melted butter or
  margarine
½ cup fine packaged dry
  bread crumbs

Sift flour with baking powder and salt. Stir in seasonings. Mix in oil and milk. Drop batter by tablespoons into melted butter then into crumbs, until coated. Arrange on top of casserole mixture. Yield: about 8-10 dumplings.

Conventional Cooking:
1. *Brown veal pieces. Combine in casserole with remaining ingredients. Bake in moderate oven, 350°, about 20 minutes.*
2. *Add dumplings. Increase heat to 400°. Cook, uncovered, 10 minutes; cover, cook 10 minutes more.*

Poultry

Once upon a time poultry was served only on Sundays and holidays. Today, with the variety of recipes available and the Radarange microwave oven to cut time and effort to a minimum, weekly menus can be much more varied and more enjoyable.

Holiday dinners were once an ordeal for the home-maker, with long hours spent in the kitchen. Now the traditional turkey can be prepared in less than one fourth the usual time. You can really enjoy the holidays this year!

Thawing poultry

Put frozen fowl in a dish in the Radarange oven, breast up. Figure about ½ minute per pound. Turn breast side down for the same length of time. Allow 15 minutes standing time for the interior temperature to equalize. Cut up, or stuff, as desired. Do not salt or use salt butter; it seems to toughen the skin.

Roasting poultry

Allow 7 minutes per pound, and turn on all four sides, if possible. Areas that seem to cook too fast should be covered by a narrow strip of foil to retard cooking by deflecting microwaves. Toward the end of the cooking time, allow the legs to stand away from the body so that the meat on the inside of the thighs will cook.

To test with a meat thermometer, always remove the fowl from the oven. (Remove the thermometer before returning the fowl to the oven.) At 183° to 185° stop cooking, allow to stand. The temperature will rise slightly in carry-over cooking.

Wait at least 15 minutes before carving.

AFRICAN GOLD COAST CHICKEN

1- to 2½-pound broiler-
  fryer, quartered
2 cups boiling water
Juice of 1 lemon
1 teaspoon salt
2 cups chopped onions
¼ cup vegetable oil
2 tablespoons tomato paste

½ tablespoon chili powder
½ teaspoon ginger
¼ teaspoon pepper
2 tablespoons cornstarch
¼ cup red wine
4 hard-cooked eggs, shelled
  and quartered

Place chicken pieces and giblets in a 2½-quart casserole; add boiling water, lemon juice, and salt. Cover, cook in Radarange oven 10 minutes, turn dish 180° after 5 minutes cooking. Pour chicken broth into a 2-cup measure. Set chicken aside in a bowl, cover. Add onions and oil to the 2½-quart casserole; cook in oven 5 minutes, stirring halfway through cooking. Stir tomato paste and seasonings into hot broth, smoothing out lumps, and add to onions in the casserole.

Cook in oven 3 minutes. Stir. Add cornstarch to red wine, stirring constantly to make a smooth paste, and add to hot chicken broth mixture. Cook in oven 1 minute, stir well. Add chicken pieces, spooning sauce over so that pieces are well coated. Cover, cook in oven 10* minutes. Turn dish 180° after 5 minutes cooking time. Add eggs, warm in oven 1 minute more. For the authentic touch, serve with fluffy hot rice and dry cottage cheese. Makes 4 servings.

*Time depends on age of chicken. It should be fork tender. You may need to cook 12 to 14 minutes.

Conventional Cooking:
1. *In large saucepan, boil 2 cups water, add chicken, lemon juice, and salt. Simmer about 30 minutes.*
2. *In medium fry pan sauté onions in oil till limp, add tomato paste, seasonings, and 2 cups of chicken broth from cooked chicken. Cook over low heat about 10 minutes.*
3. *Mix cornstarch and wine, stir well to remove all lumps. Add to hot chicken broth. Cook over low heat till thickened, stirring often.*
4. *Pour chicken broth, tomato sauce over chicken in large saucepan. Cover, cook over medium heat till chicken is fork tender, about 25 to 30 minutes.*

APRICOT BAKED CHICKEN

1 broiler-fryer (2½ to 3 pounds) cut up
¼ cup bottled Russian dressing

2 tablespoons mayonnaise
½ cup apricot preserves
½ envelope dry onion soup mix

Arrange chicken pieces in 2-quart oblong baking dish, placing thickest "meaty" pieces around edge of dish. Mix together remaining ingredients; spread mixture over chicken, coating each piece. Cover with wax paper. Cook in Radarange oven 20 minutes until fork tender, turning dish around after 10 minutes. Let stand 5 minutes, covered. Serve on noodles. Makes 4 to 5 servings.

Conventional Cooking:
1. *Arrange chicken pieces skin side up in roasting pan. Proceed as directed.*
2. *Bake in a moderate oven, 375°, about 1 hour.*

BRAISED DUCKLING SPANISH STYLE

5-pound duck, cut up	1 large tomato, thinly
¼ cup flour	sliced
2 teaspoons paprika	⅓ cup chopped stuffed
½ cup dry sherry	olives
1¾ cups chicken bouillon	2 tablespoons minced
1 onion, sliced	parsley

Heat large Browning Skillet in Radarange oven 4½ minutes. Add half the duckling pieces, skin side down. Cook, uncovered, 1 minute per side. Drain off fat, reserve. Heat Browning Skillet again 2 minutes. Add rest of duckling pieces. Cook, uncovered, 1 minute per side. Drain fat. Remove duckling to paper towels.

Return 3 tablespoons fat to skillet, heat in oven 45 seconds. Stir in flour and paprika until smooth. Gradually stir in sherry; blend in chicken bouillon, mix well with a wire whisk. Cook in oven 5 to 6 minutes, stir twice. Add browned duckling, top with sliced onion. Cover, cook in oven 20 minutes, turn dish 180° halfway through cooking. Add sliced tomato, olives, and parsley. Cook 2 minutes more. Makes 3 to 4 servings.

Conventional Cooking:
1. *Brown duckling pieces and onion. Make a sauce with flour, wine, and bouillon; pour over duckling in casserole. Top with remaining ingredients.*
2. *Cover, bake in moderate oven, 350°, about 1 hour.*

CHICKEN BREASTS WITH ARTICHOKES

3 whole chicken breasts,
    boned and skinned
Bread crumbs to coat
1 tablespoon butter or
    margarine
1 package (8 oz.) frozen
    artichoke hearts au gratin,
    partially thawed

¼ cup white wine
Salt and pepper
2 strips bacon, cooked and
    crumbled (page 75)

Cut chicken breasts in half, dip in bread crumbs to coat. Preheat 10-inch Browning Skillet 4½ minutes in Radarange oven, add butter and chicken pieces. Cook 4 minutes in oven, turning chicken pieces over halfway through cooking. Place artichoke au gratin hearts on chicken breasts. Add wine. Cover. Cook 5 to 6 minutes until vegetables are fork tender. Season to taste. Top with crumbled bacon. Makes 4 servings.

Conventional Cooking:
1. Crumb chicken pieces. Brown quickly on both sides in hot fat. Place in baking pan; top with artichoke hearts. Add wine.
2. Bake covered in a moderate oven, 350°, 45 to 55 minutes until tender. If necessary, add additional wine or butter to keep moist.

CORNISH CASSOULET

2 tablespoons vegetable oil
2 Rock Cornish hens, split
   in halves (about 1 pound
   each)
½ teaspoon seasoned
   pepper
½ pound sweet Italian
   sausage, cut up
3 tart apples, peeled and
   sliced

1 green pepper, diced
1 medium onion, chopped
1 can (1 lb. 4 oz.) white
   kidney beans, drained
¼ teaspoon Tabasco sauce
1 teaspoon Worcestershire
   sauce

Heat Browning Skillet in Radarange oven 4½ minutes.
Add oil and Cornish hen halves, breast side down, rubbed
with pepper. Cover, cook in oven 5 minutes. Turn halves
over after 2½ minutes. Remove from skillet; keep warm.
Add sausage, apples, pepper, and onion to skillet; cook in
oven 5 minutes, drain fat. Stir in beans and seasonings. Place
hens on bean mixture. Cover, cook in oven 10 to 12 minutes,
turning skillet one quarter turn every 2 minutes. Makes 4
servings.

Conventional Cooking:
1. Brown hens in hot fat. Mix together remaining ingredients
   in casserole. Place hens on top.
2. Cook in a moderate oven, 350°, about 75 minutes.

DUCKLING WITH APPLE STUFFING

1 duckling (about 5 pounds)
1 package (8 oz.) herb-
   seasoned bread stuffing
   mix
¼ cup diced celery
1 tablespoon minced parsley

1 small onion, chopped
2 tart apples, chopped
2 tablespoons honey
½ teaspoon bottled brown-
   ing sauce

114

Rinse duckling; pat dry; remove surplus fat from body cavity and neck. Put giblets in bowl with 1½ cups hot water; cook in Radarange oven 15 minutes, reserve for gravy. Prepare stuffing mix as directed on package. Add next 4 ingredients; toss well to mix. Stuff duckling, close openings with wooden picks and string. With a fork, or sharp pointed knife, prick skin every ½ inch around thigh, back, and lower breast to allow fat to cook out. Tie legs to tail; tie wings close to body. Cover wings and small end of legs and tail with small pieces of foil. Place duckling, breast side up, on Radarange Cooking Grill set in its own 2-quart baking pan. Cook in oven 22 minutes; turn dish at end of 10 minutes; at same time brush top of duckling with mixture 2 tablespoons honey and ½ teaspoon browning sauce. Drain off pan drippings, reserve. Turn duckling breast side down on grill. Cook in oven 22 minutes, turn dish at end of 10 minutes, and at same time brush surface of duckling with remaining honey glaze. Turn duckling breast side up. When the bird is done the legs will move freely, and leg and thigh meat will pierce tender with a fork. Let stand 15 minutes before carving. For a crisp skin, slide duckling under conventional broiler for about 2 minutes. Makes 4 to 5 servings.

Gravy:

4 tablespoons drippings	¼ cup white wine
1¾ cup giblet broth	Giblets, chopped
1 can (3 oz.) sliced broiled mushrooms	Salt, pepper to taste

Remove duckling and rack from pan. Pour off most of fat, leaving about 4 tablespoons drippings. Blend in 4 tablespoons flour to make a smooth paste. Measure broth from giblets, add liquid from 1 can (3 oz.) sliced broiled mushrooms and enough hot water (if necessary) to make 2 cups. Gradually add liquid to pan, stir smooth. Cook in Radarange oven 1½ minutes, stirring at 30 second intervals. Add ¼ cup white wine, mushrooms, and finely chopped giblets. Season to taste with salt and pepper. Mix well, cook in oven 1½ to 2 minutes, until thick and smooth. Stir at 30 second intervals. Makes about 2½ cups.

Conventional Cooking:

1. *Bake stuffed duck in 325° oven. After 1½ hours, pour off excess fat, then baste duck with 2 tablespoons honey.*
2. *Bake half an hour longer.*

To make gravy:

1. *Simmer giblets in 1½ cups water about 1 hour or till tender.*
2. *Mix ingredients as above; cook in saucepan over low heat, stirring constantly, until gravy becomes bubbly and brown.*

DUCKLING BORDEAUX

3½- to 4½-pound duck-
  ling, quartered
½ cup orange marmalade
1 tablespoon soy sauce
1 tablespoon butter

2 tablespoons flour
¾ cup white wine
1 tablespoon vinegar
⅓ cup chicken broth
¼ teaspoon pepper

Remove excess fat from duckling pieces. Place duckling on plastic cooking rack in 2-quart utility dish. Cover with paper toweling. Cook in Radarange oven 10 minutes, turn dish 180° after 5 minutes cooking time. Drain off fat. Mix marmalade and soy sauce. Reserve ¼ cup of the mixture for sauce, use remainder to baste duckling. Cook 10 minutes more in oven, turning dish 180° after 5 minutes. Drain fat. To prepare sauce; melt butter in oven 30 seconds, stir in flour. Add all remaining ingredients. Stir, cook in oven 2 minutes. Stir with a wire whisk. Cook 30 seconds more, stir. Pour sauce over duckling, cook in oven 5 minutes more. Makes 2 to 4 servings.

Conventional Cooking:

1. *Brown duckling pieces in heavy skillet.*
2. *Transfer to oven-proof casserole. Baste duckling with ¼ cup marmalade mixed with soy sauce. Roast in moderate oven, 350°, about 45 minutes, or until fork tender. Drain off fat.*
3. *Prepare sauce, pour over duckling before serving.*

EASY TURKEY BROCCOLI BAKE

2 packages (10 oz. each)
frozen chopped broccoli,
thawed and drained
1 envelope dry onion soup
mix
1 cup dairy sour cream
2 cups diced cooked turkey

1 cup whipping cream,
softly whipped
1 tablespoon grated Parmesan cheese
Buttered Bread Crumbs
(page 223)

Spread broccoli in 2-quart oblong baking pan. Cover with water, cook in Radarange oven 7 minutes; drain. Stir soup mix into sour cream; spread ½ mixture over broccoli. Top with diced turkey. Fold whipped cream into remaining soup/sour cream mixture; spoon over turkey. Cover, cook in oven 10 minutes, turning dish halfway through cooking time. Mix cheese and crumbs, sprinkle over casserole. Cook 1 minute longer. Makes 6 servings.

Conventional Cooking:
1. Prepare ingredients as directed, layer into casserole.
2. Bake covered in a moderate oven, 350°, 25 to 30 minutes.

ELEGANT GAME HENS

4 Rock Cornish hens (about
1 pound each)
Stuffing*
2 tablespoons lemon juice
2 tablespoons grenadine

syrup
2 tablespoons oil
1 teaspoon bottled brown-
ing sauce

Rinse and dry hens. Stuff; tie legs together close to body with string. Mix next 4 ingredients, reserving half for basting. Spread half over hens. Place on a large platter; cook in Radarange oven, breast side down for 15 minutes. Turn hens breast side up, baste them. Turn dish 180°, cook 15 minutes more. Remove from oven, let stand, insert meat thermometer. Cover hens with foil to keep warm for about 8 minutes before serving. Temperature should read 185°. Makes 4 servings.

117

*Stuffing:

½ cup hot water	1 egg, beaten
2 tablespoons butter or margarine	½ cup crushed pineapple, drained
½ package (4 oz.) bread stuffing mix	¼ cup chopped walnuts

Combine all ingredients, mix well. Makes enough to lightly stuff 4 hens.

Conventional Cooking:
1. Prepare hens as directed. Arrange side by side in roasting pan.
2. Roast and baste in moderate oven, 350°, about 1 hour, or until done.

FRUITED DUCKLING

4- to 5-pound duckling, skinned	2 tablespoons oil
1 tablespoon bottled browning sauce	1 cup canned peach nectar*
¼ teaspoon instant minced garlic	2 tablespoons cornstarch
½ teaspoon salt	¾ to 1 cup mixed dried fruit (soaked for 30 minutes in warm water to cover)
2 tablespoons butter or margarine	

Remove skin from duck. (Use a sharp pointed knife to cut through skin along center of breast bone from neck to vent. Pull skin away from body, loosening by running knife underneath the fat close to the meat.) Remove excess fat.

Quarter duckling, brush pieces with mixed seasoning and melted butter. Let stand 1 hour. Heat large Browning Skillet in Radarange oven 4½ minutes. Add oil and duckling pieces.

Cook in oven 4 minutes, turning pieces after 2 minutes. Add peach nectar. Cover, cook in oven on defrost or slow-cook cycle for 30 minutes. Turn duck pieces over after 15 minutes.

* Or use any other favorite fruit flavor.

118

Remove duck from skillet. Mix cornstarch with a little cold water, add to sauce in skillet, stir well. Add drained fruit to sauce, cook in oven 3 minutes, stirring after 1½ minutes. Return duck to skillet, spooning sauce over pieces. Cover, cook 5 minutes longer. Makes 4 servings.

Conventional Cooking:
1. *Skin duckling and season. Brown in hot fat. Place in casserole, add sauce and drained fruit.*
2. *Cook covered until tender in moderate oven, 375°, about 1 hour.*

MEXICAN CHICKEN

3½ to 4 pounds chicken parts
1 tablespoon chili powder
¼ teaspoon pepper
¼ teaspoon cinnamon
1 teaspoon salt
¼ cup chopped onion
1 cup pineapple juice*

1 can (1 lb. 4 oz.) pineapple chunks
2 bananas, sliced lengthwise
1 ripe avocado, sliced
½ pound seedless white grapes, in clusters
2 tablespoons cornstarch

Place chicken pieces in 2-quart oblong pan. Mix the seasonings, onion, and juice, pour over chicken. Cover, cook in Radarange oven 12 minutes. Spread pineapple chunks on top. Turn dish 180°, cook 10 to 12 minutes more, covered. Remove chicken and pineapple to serving dish; garnish with fruit. Thicken pan gravy (about 2 cups) with 2 tablespoons cornstarch, cook 1½ minutes; serve separately. Makes 6 servings.

*Drain juice from chunks, reserve 1 cup.

Conventional Cooking:
1. *Brown chicken pieces in ¼ cup hot oil in Dutch oven or chicken fryer. Pour off oil. Combine seasonings and onion with 1 cup water and juice; pour over chicken pieces. Top with pineapple chunks.*
2. *Bake, covered, in moderate oven, 375°, about 45 minutes. Remove cover, continue cooking an additional 15 to 20 minutes. Garnish with fruit.*

NEW STYLE BAKED TURKEY

1 cup melted butter or
  margarine
Salt and pepper
1 tablespoon paprika
1 teaspoon bottled browning
  sauce

1 fryer-roaster turkey (4 to
  5 pounds) cut up
1 teaspoon packaged herb-
  seasoned bread stuffing
  mix, finely crushed

Melt butter in small bowl in Radarange oven 1 minute 45 seconds. Combine with salt, pepper, paprika, and browning sauce. Roll turkey parts first in butter, then crumbs. On large baking dish, place thick meaty pieces on outer edge of dish, legs and wings in center. (Reserve backs and cook later.) Drizzle with any remaining butter mixture, cover with paper towels. Cook in oven 15 minutes, turn dish 180° and cook 10 minutes longer, until fork tender. Cook remaining back pieces 5 to 6 minutes in oven. Makes 8 servings.

Conventional Cooking:
1. Prepare turkey pieces as directed. Place in roasting pan, and drizzle with remaining basting mixture.
2. Cover, bake in a moderate oven, 350°, about 1½ hours, or until tender.

"QUICKIE" CHICKEN WITH STUFFING

4 whole chicken breasts
  (about 3 pounds)
1 package (8 oz.) bread
  stuffing mix
1 can (10½ oz.) chicken
  gravy
¼ cup minced onions

1 tablespoon butter
¼ cup sherry
¼ cup canned tomato sauce
1 teaspoon instant minced
  parsley
¼ teaspoon rosemary

Skin and bone chicken breasts, split. Prepare stuffing mix as directed on package. Spread in shallow 2-quart baking pan. Place chicken pieces on stuffing. Sauté onions with butter in small bowl 1½ minutes in Radarange oven. Mix with remaining ingredients; pour over chicken. Cover with plastic film wrap. Cook in oven 12 minutes, turning dish completely around once. Chicken should be fork tender. Let stand a few minutes before serving. Cut in squares to serve. Makes 4 to 6 servings.

Conventional Cooking:
1. *Prepare moist stuffing mix as directed on package. Arrange split breasts in layer on stuffing. Mix remaining ingredients, pour over chicken. Cover with foil.*
2. *Bake in a moderate oven, 350°, 45 to 55 minutes, removing foil during last 10 minutes of cooking.*

ROAST CHICKEN

5-pound roasting chicken
1 tablespoon shortening
1 teaspoon paprika

1 teaspoon bottled browning sauce
½ cup white wine or sherry

Truss chicken, place in shallow oblong baking pan. Mix together remaining ingredients in a glass measuring cup; cover, heat in Radarange oven 1 minute. Baste chicken with warm mixture. Cook chicken in oven, breast side down, 8 minutes; turn on one wing, baste, cook 8 minutes more. Roll chicken on the other wing, baste, cook in oven 8 minutes more. Turn chicken breast side up, baste, cook 6 to 8 minutes more. Let stand 10 to 15 minutes. Test with thermometer in meaty part of breast. Temperature should be between 180° and 185°. Makes 8 servings.

Conventional Cooking:
1. *Prepare bird as directed.*
2. *Roast in a moderate oven, 325°, basting several times, about 3 to 3½ hours until done.*

ROAST TURKEY

13- to 14-pound young turkey (refrigerator
  temperature)
Salt
2 apples, quartered,
  cored

Poultry seasoning
1 tablespoon bottled browning sauce
2 tablespoons shortening
1 tablespoon paprika
2 tablespoons flour

Sprinkle turkey cavity with salt. Roll apples in poultry seasoning, sprinkle with browning sauce; place in turkey cavity. Truss turkey, rub all over with blended shortening and paprika. Place turkey in plastic roasting bag with 2 tablespoons flour and secure with string. Pierce bag several times with kitchen fork, place turkey on large glass or earthenware dish. Cook in Radarange oven as follows:

Breast up—20 to 22 minutes
1st side—20 to 22 minutes
2nd side—20 to 22 minutes
Back up—19 to 21 minutes

Remove turkey from oven, insert meat thermometer through bag to center of breast. Let stand until thermometer reaches 180° to 185°. Carefully slit bag and remove bird to warm platter. Use liquid in bag to make gravy. Makes 10 to 12 servings.

Conventional Cooking:
1. Prepare bird as directed.
2. Roast in a slow moderate oven, 325°, until tender, about 5 hours.

SWEET AND SOUR CHICKEN

1 tablespoon cornstarch
1 tablespoon cold water
½ cup sugar
¼ cup wine vinegar
½ cup soy sauce
¼ teaspoon garlic powder
¼ teaspoon coarsely ground
  black pepper

1 tablespoon mixed pickling
  spices
3 tablespoons butter or
  margarine
3¼ to 3½ pounds best of
  the fryer chicken parts or
  2 broiler-fryers, split

122

Mix together first 8 ingredients in bowl or 1-quart casserole. Cook in Radarange oven 1 minute, stir well. Continue cooking 1½ minutes more. Stir.

Melt butter in 2-quart oblong baking dish 45 seconds in oven. Place chicken in dish, skin side down; baste well with sauce. Cover with plastic film and cook 12 minutes. Turn pieces over and baste with remaining sauce. Cover again and cook in oven 12 minutes more or until chicken is fork tender. Makes 4 servings.

Conventional Cooking:
1. *Melt butter in shallow casserole. Arrange chicken in single layer. Brush with sauce.*
2. *Bake in moderate oven, 350°, turning pieces in pan and brushing often with sauce. Bake almost 1 hour, or until tender.*

TURKEY A LA KING

1 tablespoon butter or margarine	*¼ cup dry sherry*
1 cup sliced mushrooms	*½ cup sliced canned pimientos*
1 medium green pepper, slivered	*3 cups hot medium White Sauce (page 235)*
5 to 6 cups cubed cooked turkey	*Salt and pepper*

Melt butter in 2½-quart casserole in Radarange oven 30 seconds. Stir in mushrooms and green pepper; cook in oven 3 minutes. Add remaining ingredients, mix well; cover. Cook in oven 5 minutes. Stir; let stand 5 minutes before serving. Makes 8 servings.

Serve on toast, toasted English muffins, or split hot biscuits.

Conventional Cooking:
1. *Sauté mushrooms and green pepper in butter. Make medium white sauce (see page 235). Combine all ingredients in casserole.*
2. *Bake in medium oven, 350°, about 20 minutes, or mix ingredients in saucepan. Cook over medium heat about 10 minutes until heated.*

Fish and Seafood

Some people *think* they don't like fish because they have never tasted any that was properly cooked! When fish is cooked by ordinary methods it can be overdone, dry, and tasteless. Fish and seafood cooked in the Radarange microwave oven have a delicate flavor and are moist, tender, and flaky. Your family will be surprised and delighted with any one of these recipes. Just be careful not to overcook—follow directions exactly.

Frozen fish fillets may be partially *defrosted in your Radarange oven by placing the frozen package (unless wrapped in foil) on a paper towel laid in the oven. Turn package at least once during thawing. A 1-pound package of fish fillets will defrost sufficiently in about 2 minutes to allow* separating the pieces under cold running water. Longer heating in the oven may result in partial cooking of the outer portions and is undesirable. Always cook frozen fish shortly after defrosting. Stack fillets so fish has uniform thickness. Cook fish only until it can be flaked with a fork.

Shrimp, crab, lobster, and other shellfish are especially good when cooked in the Radarange oven.

BAKED CLAMS AND RICE

2 cups hot milk
6 tablespoons butter or margarine, divided
¼ cup flour
½ teaspoon salt
⅛ teaspoon seasoned pepper
Pinch thyme

½ cup tomato paste
2 (8 oz.) cans minced clams and juice
3 cups cooked rice (page 221)
⅓ cup soft bread crumbs
2 tablespoons grated sharp cheese

Warm milk in Radarange oven 2½ minutes. Measure 4 tablespoons butter into glass bowl; cook in oven 45 seconds. Blend in flour and seasonings. Gradually stir in hot milk. Cook in oven 1½ minutes, stir; cook 30 seconds to 1 minute longer. Mix in tomato paste and clams with their juice. Cook in oven 1 minute longer, stir well. Alternate layers of rice and clam mixture in 2-quart casserole. Melt remaining butter, mix with bread crumbs and cheese. Sprinkle over top. Cook in oven 8 to 9 minutes, turning casserole a quarter turn every 3 minutes. Makes 6 servings.

Conventional Cooking:
1. Make a sauce with first 7 ingredients. Stir in clams. Prepare casserole as directed.
2. Bake in moderate oven, 350°, about 25 to 30 minutes.

CHINESE RICE AND CRAB

2 tablespoons vegetable oil
1 green onion, chopped
(tops included)
¼ cup finely chopped celery
½ cup chopped canned
mushrooms, drained
2 eggs, beaten
1 tablespoon water

1 teaspoon salt
Dash seasoned pepper
1 teaspoon minced parsley
1 can (6½ oz.) crabmeat*
flaked
3 cups freshly cooked hot
rice
2 tablespoons soy sauce

Preheat large Browning Skillet in Radarange oven 2½ minutes. Add oil and vegetables. Cook 2 minutes, stir halfway through cooking time. Beat eggs with water, salt, pepper, and parsley. Add beaten eggs to vegetables; cook 2½ minutes. Use a fork to shred thin layer of cooked egg into small pieces. Add crabmeat and rice, mix thoroughly. Sprinkle with soy sauce; mix well. Cook in oven 4 minutes, stirring at 2-minute intervals. Makes 4 servings.

*Other canned fish may be substituted for crabmeat.

Conventional Cooking:
1. Heat oil in skillet, cook eggs. Shred eggs and add vege-tables. Cook few minutes until onions are translucent. Add remaining ingredients and mix well.
2. Bake in moderate oven 350°, 6 to 15 minutes.

CREAMED FINNAN HADDIE

2 pounds finnan haddie*
2 cups boiling water
6 tablespoons butter or
margarine
2 tablespoons minced green
pepper
2 tablespoons minced onion

2 tablespoons minced
canned pimiento
1 teaspoon paprika
6 tablespoons flour
1 tall can (13 oz.)
evaporated milk

126

Place finnan haddie in shallow baking dish. Add boiling water. Cover with plastic wrap, cook in Radarange oven 6 minutes. Let stand while preparing sauce. Melt butter in 2-quart casserole in oven for 1 minute. Stir in green pepper, onion, and minced pimiento. Cook in oven 4 minutes, stirring twice. Stir in paprika and flour until smooth. Add milk gradually, stirring constantly. Cook in oven 1 minute. Drain fish, reserving stock (water in which it cooked). Measure 1⅓ cups stock into sauce. Stir until blended and smooth. Cook in oven 4 minutes, stirring 3 to 4 times. Add finnan haddie flaked into pieces. Cook in oven 2 to 3 minutes, until heated through. Serve with Baked Potatoes (page 161) or mashed potatoes. Makes 6 servings.

*Traditionally, finnan haddie is smoked haddock. Smoked cod is often sold as finnan haddie and can be used in its place.

Conventional Cooking:
1. *Poach fish in a large skillet after water has come to a simmer. Heat about 10 minutes.*
2. *Sauté vegetables in butter in saucepan over medium heat. Make white sauce with remaining ingredients. Add 1⅓ cups fish stock to sauce.*
3. *Combine all in casserole, cover, bake in 350° oven 30 minutes.*

CREOLE HALIBUT

¼ cup butter or margarine
1 onion, chopped
½ cup chopped green pepper
¼ cup finely chopped celery
1 garlic clove, minced
1 can (1 lb.) stewed tomatoes
1 can (3 oz.) sliced broiled mushrooms, drained

½ teaspoon sugar
1 teaspoon salt
Dash Tabasco sauce (or more to taste)
4 portions halibut steaks (about 1–1½ pounds)
Chopped parsley
Lemon wedges

127

Combine butter, onion, green pepper, celery, and garlic in bowl or small casserole. Cook in Radarange oven 3 minutes, stirring 3 times. Add tomatoes, mushrooms, and seasonings. Cover, cook in oven 5 minutes; stir. Arrange halibut in greased shallow baking dish. Pour sauce over fish. Cook in oven 8 to 10 minutes or until fish flakes easily with a fork. Let stand, covered, few minutes before serving. Garnish with parsley and lemon wedges. Makes 4 servings.

Conventional Cooking:
1. *Prepare sauce, cooking over medium heat about 15 minutes. Pour over fish in casserole.*
2. *Bake in a moderate oven, 350°, about 35 minutes.*

CRUMBED SALMON STEAKS

½ cup butter or margarine
½ teaspoon paprika
1 tablespoon lemon juice
6 salmon steaks
  (2½ pounds*)
1½ cups corn flakes
  crumbs

1 teaspoon salt
½ teaspoon dill weed
Chopped parsley
Lemon wedges

Melt butter in 2-quart oblong dish in Radarange oven 45 seconds. Stir in paprika and lemon juice. Dip the salmon steaks in the hot butter, roll in cereal crumbs mixed with seasoning.

Cook 3 salmon steaks in the 2-quart oblong dish or on a large platter in the oven 4 minutes. Turn the dish around after 2 minutes of cooking time. Fish should flake easily with a fork when done. Cook 1 more minute if not done. Repeat same cooking time with 3 remaining salmon steaks. Sprinkle with parsley, serve with lemon wedges. Makes 6 servings.

*Steaks are about ¾-inch thick.

Conventional Cooking:
1. *Dip steaks in melted butter, then roll in seasoned crumbs. Arrange in shallow baking dish.*
2. *Bake in a slow moderate oven, 325°, about 35 minutes until fish flakes easily with a fork.*

Succulent, golden brown duckling, stuffed with a savory mixture that includes celery, onion, apples, and wine. This bird will grace any table with its beauty and flavor (page 114).

Garnish a gleaming glazed pork roast with halved slices of canned pineapple and rosy red canned crab apples. Magnificent! (page 84).

For dinner "a deux" try these hearty handsome Beef Kabobs (page 77). Serve with baked potatoes (page 161) and raw vegetable relishes.

Serve this hearty Gourmet Beef Stew (page 86) on a night when the air is nippy and appetites robust.

Below, hot French bread is good with this Veal Scaloppine Milano (page 106) which is sure to become a favorite at your house when you prepare it this flavorful way.

You'll love this brand new way to make an old favorite—Chow Mein with Beef Heart (page 80).

Lobster Tails (page 133) cooked to perfection in just three minutes! A delightful main dish for an extra special dinner.

FAVORITE FILLETS

1 bay leaf
1 tablespoon mayonnaise
1 tablespoon prepared
 mustard
1 can (8 oz.) tomato sauce
1 pound flounder fillets,
 fresh or frozen

2 tablespoons butter or
 margarine
½ cup seasoned bread
 crumbs

Combine bay leaf, mayonnaise, mustard, and tomato sauce in bowl. Heat in Radarange oven 2 minutes. Arrange fish fillets in single layer in greased shallow 2½-quart baking dish. Pour hot sauce over fish, dot with butter, and sprinkle with crumbs. Cook in oven 4 minutes until fish flakes easily with a fork. Turn dish 180° after 2 minutes of cooking time. Makes 4 servings.

Conventional Cooking:
1. Combine first 4 ingredients, cook over medium heat in saucepan until hot throughout.
2. Grease a 2-quart casserole. Arrange fish fillets. Cover with hot sauce, butter, and crumbs. Bake in 350° oven for 30 to 35 minutes.

FILLETS THERMIDOR

½ cup light cream
1 cup mayonnaise
1 can (4 oz.) canned mushroom stems and pieces
¼ cup dry sherry
1½ pounds frozen fish
   fillets, thawed

Salt and pepper
⅓ cup soft bread crumbs
⅓ cup grated Parmesan
   cheese
2 tablespoons soft butter or
   margarine
Paprika

Stir cream and mayonnaise together until smooth. Add mushrooms and sherry; mix well. Spoon ½ the sauce into shallow oblong 2-quart baking dish sprayed with vegetable oil coating. Layer fish fillets on sauce, sprinkle with salt and pepper; cover with remaining sauce. Mix crumbs and cheese. Sprinkle over sauce. Dot with butter; cover with plastic film wrap. Cook in oven 7 to 8 minutes, turning dish 180° after 4 minutes. Fish should flake easily when tested with a fork. Sprinkle with paprika for color, before serving. Makes 4 servings.

Conventional Cooking:
1. *Prepare fish in greased casserole, layering sauce and fish.*
2. *Bake in 325° oven for about 35 minutes.*

FISH CASSEROLE FLORENTINE

1 can (1 lb.) salmon*
2 cups cooked spinach,
   drained
2 cups grated cheddar
   cheese

2 cups thick White Sauce
   (page 235)
½ cup toasted Buttered
   Bread Crumbs (page 223)

Drain and flake salmon. Chop spinach. Arrange alternate layers salmon and spinach in greased 1-quart casserole. Stir cheese in hot white sauce. Pour hot sauce into casserole, lifting layers with a fork to distribute sauce. Top with crumbs. Cook in Radarange oven 5 to 6 minutes turning dish twice, a quarter turn. Let stand 5 minutes. Makes 4 servings.

*Other canned fish or shellfish (same weight) may be substituted for salmon. Inexpensive canned mackerel is very good in this recipe.

Conventional Cooking:
1. Prepare casserole as directed.
2. Bake in moderate oven, 350°, 30 to 35 minutes until browned and bubbling hot.

FISH COSTA BRAVA

1½ pounds flounder fillets*
Salt, pepper, paprika
Flour
2 tablespoons vegetable oil
¼ teaspoon garlic powder
2 tablespoons lemon juice
1 small onion, minced
2 tablespoons minced parsley

1 can (8 oz.) peas, partially drained
1 large package (10½ oz.) frozen rissole (balls) potatoes, thawed
4 thin slices tomato
4 teaspoons butter or margarine

Cut fish into 4 serving pieces to fit a 2-quart oblong baking dish. Sprinkle pieces with seasonings, dip lightly in flour. Mix together oil, garlic, and lemon juice in a custard cup. Heat in Radarange oven 1 minute. Stir and pour over and around fish. Cover with plastic film wrap, cook in oven 4 minutes. Mix together onion, parsley, and peas with liquid, mashing the peas slightly. Spread over fish. Arrange potato balls around fish, top each piece of fish with a tomato slice, dot with butter; cook in oven 3 to 4 minutes, covered, turning dish 180° after 2 minutes. Cook till fish flakes easily with a fork. Makes four servings.

*Cod, haddock, or other white fish fillets may be used.

Conventional Cooking:

1. *Prepare fish as directed, and top with remaining ingredients.*
2. *Bake in moderate oven, 350°, about 30 minutes until fish flakes easily with fork. During last 10 minutes of cooking cover with a piece of foil to prevent top drying out.*

FISH UNDER A BLANKET

3 tablespoons butter or margarine, divided	*¼ pound fresh mushrooms, finely chopped*
2½ pounds halibut steaks,* drained and dried	*¼ cup finely chopped celery*
2 strips bacon, chopped	*2 tablespoons minced ham*
1 carrot, finely chopped	*Salt and pepper*
1 onion, finely chopped	*¾ cup dry white wine*

Preheat large Browning Skillet 4½ minutes in Radarange oven. Add half the butter and two halibut steaks; cook in oven 1 minute, turning fish after 30 seconds. Remove browned fish and butter to 2-quart utility dish, cover. Wipe skillet out with paper towel. Heat skillet 1 minute in oven; add remaining butter and fish. Cook 1 minute, turning after 30 seconds. Add browned fish and butter to fish in casserole, making one layer. Mix together bacon, prepared vegetables, and ham in skillet. Cook in oven 5 minutes, stir halfway through cooking time. Salt and pepper fish. Add cooked vegetables, bacon, and ham to top of fish, pour on wine. Cover with plastic film, cook 4 minutes. Turn dish 180° and cook 4 minutes more until fish flakes easily with a fork. (Time will depend on thickness of fish.) Serve with sauce from dish. Makes 5 to 6 servings.

*Or use cod, or any firm white fish.

Conventional Cooking:

1. *Sear fish on both sides in hot fat in fry pan. Combine remaining ingredients in saucepan, bring to a boil. Reduce heat and simmer 10 minutes.*
2. *Turn into a casserole, place vegetables on top. Bake in moderate oven, 350°, about 35 minutes.*

132

LOBSTER TAILS

1 package (10 oz.) frozen lobster tails	2 tablespoons melted butter
	1 teaspoon lemon juice

If lobster tails are frozen, unwrap and place in shallow glass utility dish. Heat in Radarange oven 2½ minutes. Let stand at room temperature for about 10 minutes, until lobster tails are defrosted. Make a cut lengthwise down the back, through hard shell: hold tail in both hands and open flat. Turn tails meat side up in dish. Brush with melted butter and lemon juice, and cook in Radarange oven for 2½ to 3 minutes.

Conventional Cooking:
1. Prepare thawed tails as directed.
2. Broil 10 to 15 minutes. Serve hot.

MARYLAND CASSEROLE

2 tablespoons butter or margarine	1 cup light cream
2 tablespoons flour	2 eggs, beaten
1 teaspoon salt	3 cups coarsely crumbled soda crackers
1 teaspoon paprika	18 oysters
Dash pepper	1 pound deveined shrimp,* cooked
1 cup milk	

Make White Sauce (p. 235) using first 7 ingredients. Add hot white sauce slowly to eggs; mix well. Spread a layer of crumbs in shallow 1½-quart greased baking dish; add oysters;

133

scatter with crumbs. Add shrimp; top with crumbs. Pour hot sauce over all. Cook in Radarange oven 8 minutes, turning dish a quarter turn every 2 minutes. Cover; let stand 10 minutes before serving. Makes 6 servings.

*Canned or frozen shrimp may be used.

Conventional Cooking:
1. *Combine ingredients and prepare casserole as indicated above.*
2. *Cover, bake in a moderate oven, 350°, about 30 to 35 minutes.*

POACHED CODFISH STEAKS

1 cup hot water	2 tablespoons butter
1 onion, sliced	2 tablespoons flour
1 teaspoon salt	¼ cup prepared mustard
1 bay leaf	1 tablespoon mayonnaise
¼ teaspoon lemon-pepper	1 tablespoon lemon juice
3 to 4 whole cloves	Dash Tabasco sauce
2 pounds fresh codfish steaks (4 steaks)	

Mix water, onion, and seasonings in shallow 2-quart baking dish. Cook in Radarange oven 4 minutes. Place fish in single layer in hot mixture; cover with plastic film. Cook in oven 6 minutes; turn dish 180° after 3 minutes. Cook until fish flakes easily with a fork. Strain liquid into 2 cup measure; if necessary add enough hot water to make 1¼ cups. Melt butter in small bowl in oven 30 seconds. Blend in flour to make a smooth paste. Gradually add fish liquid, stirring until smooth. Cook in oven 1 minute; stir. Add remaining ingredients; stir smooth. Cook in oven 1 minute, stirring smooth. Place fish on serving dish, or individual plates. Spoon sauce onto fish. Makes 4 servings.

Conventional Cooking:
1. *Prepare recipe as directed using a skillet big enough to hold fish without squeezing.*
2. *Cover and simmer over low heat about 20 minutes or until fish flakes easily with a fork.*

134

POACHED FILLETS VERMOUTH

1 bunch scallions trimmed
  and sliced thin (about 1
  cup)
1½ pounds flounder or
  perch fillets
1 teaspoon salt

Dash black pepper
¾ teaspoon dill weed
⅔ cup dry vermouth
¼ cup slivered toasted
  almonds
Paprika

In a shallow baking dish (1½ or 2 quart) sprayed with vegetable oil coating, spread scallions. Arrange fish fillets in single layer over scallions, sprinkle with seasonings, add vermouth. Cover with plastic film wrap, cook in Radarange oven 5 to 6 minutes until fish flakes easily with a fork. Let stand, covered, about 3 minutes. Scatter with almonds and sprinkle with paprika. Makes 4 servings.

Conventional Cooking:
1. *Arrange fish as directed.*
2. *Cook about 15 to 20 minutes in moderate oven, 350°, until fish flakes easily with a fork.*

POLISH KOLETKI

3 thin slices white bread,
  trimmed
⅓ cup milk
1 can (7½–8 oz.) salmon,
  drained

3 tablespoons melted butter,
  or margarine
⅛ teaspoon pepper
½ teaspoon nutmeg
1 tablespoon oil

Break the bread into small pieces, add milk; let stand 10 minutes. Add flaked salmon and remaining ingredients (except oil). Beat thoroughly with a fork. Chill mixture until it is easy to handle, shape into 4 cakes. Dust cakes lightly with flour. Heat a large Browning Skillet in Radarange oven, 4½ minutes. Add 1 tablespoon oil and fish cakes; cook in oven 1 minute. Turn cakes, cook in oven 1 minute more. Makes 2 servings.

Special sauce:

Pare ½ large cucumber, cut in paper-thin slices; sprinkle with salt and pepper. Combine with 1 container plain yogurt. Serve over fish cakes. Makes about 1¼ cups.

Conventional Cooking:
1. *Melt shortening in hot skillet. Brown cakes on both sides over medium heat.*
2. *Reduce heat to low and cook cakes 3 to 4 minutes without turning.*

SALMON STUFFED GREEN PEPPERS

4 large green peppers
⅓ cup mayonnaise
2 tablespoons lemon juice
⅛ teaspoon Tabasco sauce
2 tablespoons prepared
    mustard
¼ teaspoon salt

1 egg, beaten
1 cup soft bread crumbs
½ cup finely diced celery
1 tablespoon minced onion
1 can (1 lb.) salmon,
    drained and flaked
2 slices process cheese

Cut a slice from top of each pepper to make straight edge; dice slices. Remove seeds and membranes. Cook peppers 5 minutes in Radarange oven in a cooking bag folded under peppers to close. Let stand a few minutes before removing from bag. Thoroughly mix all remaining ingredients (except cheese), including diced green pepper. Fill pepper shells with mixture; stand upright in 1½- to 2-quart shallow baking dish. Cook in oven 10 to 12 minutes, turning dish 180° 3 times.

Have cheese ready-cut into 8 strips. Crisscross 2 strips cheese on top each filled hot pepper. Heat 30 seconds more in oven. Makes 4 servings.

Conventional Cooking:
1. *Prepare and fill pepper shells as directed.*
2. *Bake in a moderate oven, 375°, 35 to 45 minutes depending on size of peppers.*

SAVORY SHRIMP

2 packages (3 oz. each) cream cheese (at room temperature)
½ cup crumbled blue cheese (at room temperature)
2 tablespoons minced black olives
2 canned pimientoes, finely chopped

1 tablespoon grated onion
Dash seasoned pepper
4 medium firm ripe tomatoes, halved crossway
Salt and pepper
1 pound shrimp, cooked and cleaned
8 slices lemon

Mash cheeses together to a paste. Add olives, pimiento, onion, and pepper, whip until fluffy. Place tomato halves in 2-quart oblong baking dish; sprinkle with salt and pepper. Arrange shrimp on tomato halves, spoon cheese mixture on shrimp; top with lemon slices. Cook in Radarange oven 3½ minutes, turn dish 180°, cook 3½ minutes more. Let stand few seconds before serving. Makes 4 servings.

Conventional Cooking:
1. *Prepare ingredients as indicated. Arrange in shallow casserole as directed.*
2. *Bake in a moderate oven, 350°, 30 to 35 minutes.*

SHRIMP TOLEDO

¼ cup butter or margarine
1 garlic clove, minced
1½ pounds large shrimp,
   peeled and deveined
½ teaspoon salt

Dash seasoned pepper
1 to 2 teaspoons shrimp
   seasoning (optional)
½ cup chopped parsley

Melt butter, and sauté garlic in a small covered bowl, in Radarange oven for 30 seconds. Preheat large Browning Skillet in oven 2½ minutes. Add shrimp, stir well. Pour garlic butter over shrimp, stirring to coat. Cook 2 to 3 minutes until all shrimp are pink. Stir every minute. Sprinkle with seasonings and parsley. Serve hot. Makes 4 servings. (12 hors d'oeuvre servings.)

Conventional Cooking:
1. *Prepare shrimp as directed. Heat butter and garlic in fry pan, add shrimp.*
2. *Stir and cook shrimp over medium heat until pink, about 12 to 15 minutes. Toss with seasonings and serve hot.*

TEXAS CRAB CASSEROLE

2 cups hot medium White
   Sauce (page 235)
1 cup grated sharp cheddar
   cheese
2 egg yolks, beaten
2 cups crabmeat, fresh or
   canned

¼ cup toasted Buttered
   Bread Crumbs (page 223)
2 tablespoons grated Par-
   mesan cheese
2 tablespoons soft butter or
   margarine

Mix hot White Sauce and cheese in 1½-quart casserole; cook in Radarange oven ½ minute until cheese is completely melted, stirring after 15 seconds. Add some cheese sauce to beaten egg yolks, blend until smooth. Repeat until there is about 1 cup blended sauce and egg yolk mixture. Return to casserole; mix thoroughly. Stir in crabmeat. Sprinkle with mixed crumbs and grated Parmesan cheese, dot with butter. Cook in oven 8 to 9 minutes until heated through. Turn casserole a quarter turn at 2 minute intervals. Makes 4 servings.

Conventional Cooking:
1. *Prepare and mix ingredients.*
2. *Bake, uncovered, in a moderate oven, 350°, about 30 minutes.*

TUNA SQUARE

¼ pound noodles, cooked (about 2¼ cups) (page 221)
3 hard-cooked eggs, chopped
1 can (6½ oz.) tuna, flaked
1 can (3 oz.) sliced mushrooms with liquid
3 tablespoons butter or margarine
¼ cup flour
1 teaspoon salt
¼ cup minced onion

¼ cup sweet pickle relish
Dash Tabasco sauce
1 teaspoon Worcestershire sauce
1 tablespoon lemon juice
1 cup hot chicken broth
1 cup heated evaporated milk
1½ cups crushed potato chips
Paprika

Drain and chop noodles. Mix with eggs, tuna, and mushrooms. Place butter in bowl, or 4 cup glass measure, in Radarange oven 30 seconds. Stir in flour and salt to make a smooth paste. Blend in onion, relish, and seasonings. Gradually add hot broth and evaporated milk, stirring constantly. Cook in oven 1½ minutes, stirring several times. Mix tuna mixture and sauce; toss with 2 forks to mix well. Grease 8- or 9-inch square baking dish. Spread layer of crushed chips in bottom of dish. Spoon in half the tuna mixture; sprinkle with potato chips. Repeat layers ending with potato chips. Cook in oven 10 minutes, giving dish a quarter turn every 3 minutes. Cover; let stand 5 minutes before serving. Cut in squares to serve. Makes 6 servings.

Conventional Cooking:

1. *Layer tuna mixture and chips in greased 8-inch-square baking pan.*
2. *Bake in moderate oven, 350°, 45 to 50 minutes until firm on top.*

TURBANA OF SOLE

1 package top-of-stove
  bread stuffing mix
1 tablespoon minced canned
  pimiento
¼ teaspoon savory
½ teaspoon paprika

1 small onion, minced
½ cup wheat germ
8 sole fillets* (about 2
  pounds)
¼ cup melted butter
1 teaspoon lemon juice

Place amount hot liquid and butter or margarine called for on stuffing package in a glass bowl; cook in Radarange oven 2 minutes until butter melts. Stir in stuffing mix, seasonings, and onion. Cover, let stand 5 minutes. Mix in wheat germ. Spread mixture on fillets; roll up, place seam side down, and secure with wooden picks. Place fillets in 2-quart oblong baking dish that has been sprayed with vegetable oil coating. Brush with melted butter and lemon juice, cover with wax paper or plastic wrap. Cook in oven 7 to 8 minutes (turning dish 180° after 4 minutes) or until fish can be easily flaked with a fork. Let stand 5 minutes. Delicious with Shrimp Sauce (page 233). Makes 8 servings.

*Or any thin fillet of fish such as flounder, halibut, etc.

Conventional Cooking:

1. *Prepare ingredients as directed, spread stuffing, and roll up fillets. Place in baking dish.*
2. *Bake in a slow moderate oven, 325°, 25 to 30 minutes.*

Eggs and Cheese

Eggs need a little special attention when they are cooked in the Radarange microwave oven. For example, never cook eggs in the shell. Microwave cooking is so fast that pressure can build up inside and cause an eruption.

Don't cook eggs with an unbroken yolk. The yolk is surrounded by a membrane: because the cooking is so rapid there is a chance it will erupt. A small puncture is enough and will not spoil the appearance of the egg.

Cheese does not present any special problems. Cooking times are so short that there is no chance of the cheese becoming tough or stringy.

Treat your family to some or all of the easy, good-tasting recipes that follow.

Facts to remember about cooking eggs in the Radarange oven:

1. *Do not cook eggs in the shell. The rapid heat of microwave cooking expands the air inside the shell and can cause a mini-explosion.*

2. *When eggs are poached always be sure they are completely covered with water.*

3. *When eggs are fried or poached, puncture the yolk carefully with the tines of a fork. This will break the surface membrane and prevent an eruption.*

4. *Cooked eggs continue to cook after removal from the microwave oven. Remove eggs and egg dishes from the oven while they are still underdone. Let stand, covered, to complete cooking.*

5. *When cooking eggs, place a glass of water next to the dish with the eggs. The water slows the cooking by absorbing some of the microwaves and helps the white and yolk to cook at the same rate of speed.*

6. *Cooking time will vary with the size and temperature of eggs. For example, small eggs at room temperature will cook in less time than large eggs from the refrigerator.*

ALL-IN-ONE LUNCHEON DISH

1 package (10 oz.) frozen
  chopped broccoli
½ cup butter or margarine
6 medium eggs, separated
½ cup grated Parmesan
  cheese, divided
½ cup dairy sour cream

1 teaspoon salt
⅛ teaspoon pepper
¼ cup flour
1 cup minced cooked ham*
1 can (8 oz.) peas, drained
1 can (3 oz.) sliced mushrooms, drained

Partially cook broccoli in a small covered casserole in Radarange oven 4 minutes; drain. Cream butter, egg yolks, and half the cheese. Beat in sour cream, seasonings, and flour. Beat egg whites stiff; fold in. Spread half the egg mixture in a 2-quart oblong baking dish. Sprinkle with ham and remaining cheese. Add a layer of peas, then mushrooms, and broccoli. Spread with remaining egg mixture. Cook in oven 3 minutes; turn dish completely around, cook 3 minutes more. Spread some of uncooked portion from center of dish to edges, cook 3 minutes more. Cook 2 to 3 minutes more till wooden pick inserted in center comes out clean. Cover, let stand 8 to 10 minutes before serving. Makes 6 servings.

*Spam or other luncheon meat can substitute for ham.

Conventional Cooking:
1. *Prepare as directed.*
2. *Bake in moderate over, 350°, 35 to 40 minutes, or until set.*

CHINESE SCRAMBLE

2 tablespoons butter or margarine
6 medium eggs, beaten
1 can (10 oz.) Chinese vegetables, drained
¼ cup finely chopped onion
¼ cup finely chopped green pepper
½ cup cooked rice
2 tablespoons soy sauce

Heat butter or margarine in Radarange oven in shallow 2-quart casserole 45 seconds. Add eggs and remaining ingredients; mix well. Cover; cook in oven 4 minutes, turning dish halfway around 3 times. Stir egg mixture from outside edge to center. Cook ½ to 1 minute. Let stand, covered, about 7 to 8 minutes. Makes 4 to 5 servings.

Conventional Cooking:
1. *Heat butter in heavy fry pan. Stir in remaining ingredients.*
2. *As mixture cooks, use a fork to lift and scramble in pan to desired degree of doneness. Mixture should be like scrambled eggs. Mix and cook from 10 to 15 minutes.*

EGGS DELICIOUS

½ cup hot milk
1 package (3 oz.) cream cheese, at room temperature
6 medium eggs, beaten
1 cup diced cooked ham or luncheon meat

1 large ripe tomato, cut in wedges
Salt and pepper
2 tablespoons butter or margarine

Warm milk in Radarange oven 45 seconds. Beat cream cheese until fluffy, blend in milk. Add eggs, ham, and tomato; season to taste. Heat butter in oven in 10-inch pie plate or shallow casserole for 30 seconds. Add egg mixture; cook in oven 7 to 8 minutes for very creamy eggs, stirring eggs every 2 minutes. Cook 9 to 10 minutes for firmer eggs. Serve on, or with, hot buttered toast. Makes 4 servings.

Conventional Cooking:
1. Prepare egg mixture as directed.
2. Melt butter in 10-inch skillet; cook and stir at intervals for about 10 minutes.

HAM AND CHEESE BREAD CUSTARD

6 slices firm white bread
1 can (4½ oz.) deviled ham
½ pound process cheese, shredded
1½ cups hot milk
1 tablespoon minced onion

1 tablespoon Worcestershire sauce
⅛ teaspoon pepper
½ teaspoon salt
Dash cayenne
3 medium eggs, beaten

Spread bread slices with deviled ham. Arrange alternate layers of bread and cheese in 2½-quart casserole, ending with a cheese layer. Warm milk 3 minutes in Radarange oven. Mix hot milk with onion and seasonings; pour over beaten eggs,

144

stirring constantly. Pour milk mixture over bread and cheese. Let stand 15 minutes. Cover, cook in oven 10 minutes. Turn dish one quarter turn every 2 minutes of cooking time. Let stand, covered, a few minutes before serving. Makes 4 to 5 servings.

Conventional Cooking:
1. *Prepare as directed, scalding milk first.*
2. *Bake in slow moderate oven, 325°, about 35 minutes or until set.*

HAM AND EGG PUFFS

1 can (4½ oz.) ham spread
2 English muffins, split and lightly toasted
4 medium eggs, separated

1 teaspoon prepared mustard
Salt and pepper

Spread ham mixture on muffin halves. Beat egg whites with mustard, salt, and pepper until stiff but not dry. Mound egg whites on muffin halves, leaving a well in center. Slide an egg yolk onto each well. Pierce yolk 2 or 3 times with tines of a fork. Place puffs in oblong baking dish. Cook in Radarange oven 2 to 3 minutes, depending on desired doneness. Makes 4 servings.

Conventional Cooking:
1. *Prepare as directed. It is not necessary to pierce egg yolks.*
2. *Bake in a slow oven, 325°, about 6 to 10 minutes, depending on degree of doneness desired.*

HOT EGG SALAD MEXICANO

2 tablespoons butter or
margarine
1 small green pepper,
choppped
1 small onion, chopped
2 small ripe tomatoes,
chopped

2 cups shredded iceberg
lettuce
6 medium eggs, beaten
1 teaspoon salt
⅛ teaspoon pepper
1 teaspoon chili powder (or
to taste)

Cook first 3 ingredients in a 2-quart oblong casserole in the Radarange oven 2 minutes. Stir in remaining ingredients. Cook in oven 7½ to 8 minutes, stirring every 2½ minutes of cooking time. Cover; let stand few minutes before serving.* Makes 4 servings.

*Serve with tacos or corn chips.

Conventional Cooking:
1. Heat oil in skillet. Stir in vegetables and stir-fry for about 1 minute. Stir in eggs and seasonings.
2. Cook over medium heat, stirring often, to desired doneness.

NO-CRUST QUICHE LORRAINE

10 slices bacon, cooked
and crumbled (page 75)
1 cup shredded Swiss cheese
¼ cup minced onion
4 medium eggs

1 tall can (13 oz.) evap-
orated milk
¾ teaspoon salt
¼ teaspoon sugar
Dash cayenne pepper

Sprinkle crumbled bacon, cheese, and onion in 9-inch glass pie plate. Combine remaining ingredients; beat until well blended. Pour over bacon mixture. Bake 9 minutes, giving dish a quarter turn every 3 minutes. Center will be soft; let stand 10 to 12 minutes to finish cooking. Cut in wedges to serve. Makes 4 servings: 10 to 12 appetizer servings.

Conventional Cooking:
1. *Prepare as above.*
2. *Bake in low moderate oven, 325°, about 1 hour. Quiche is done when knife inserted in middle comes out clean.*

ONION PIE

2 tablespoons butter
3 cups thinly sliced sweet Bermuda onions
1 pound cottage cheese, warmed

⅓ cup whipping cream
2 egg yolks
½ teaspoon salt
⅛ teaspoon pepper
1 baked 9" pie shell

Heat butter in Radarange oven 1 minute. Add onions; cook in oven 4 minutes, stirring at 1 minute intervals. Warm cottage cheese in oven 1 minute. Mix together cheese, cream, and egg yolks. Add seasonings. Pour into baked pie shell. Spread onions over filling. Cook 8 to 10 minutes, turning dish a quarter turn every 2 minutes. Test center with a wooden pick for doneness; it should come out clean. Let stand 10 minutes before cutting into wedges. Makes 6 servings.

Conventional Cooking:
1. *Melt butter in pan. Add onions; cook and stir over moderate heat until soft, about 4 to 5 minutes. Heat cottage cheese. Mix together cheese, egg yolks, cream, and seasonings. Turn into baked pie shell, spread onions over filling.*
2. *Bake in moderate oven, 350°, 20 to 25 minutes, until set and fairly firm to touch.*

PIPERADE

¼ cup butter
4 medium onions, thinly
    sliced
4 ripe medium tomatoes,
    peeled and chopped
4 small green peppers, cut
    in fine slivers

1 cup sliced mushrooms
¼ teaspoon marjoram
Salt and pepper
8 medium eggs,
    beaten

Heat butter in 2-quart oblong baking dish in Radarange oven 1 minute. Stir in vegetables. Cover with plastic film. Cook in oven 5 minutes, stir; cook 5 minutes more. Beat seasonings into eggs. Pour eggs into baking dish and mix gently with vegetables. Cook 4 to 5 minutes, stir. Cover, let stand few minutes before serving. Makes 6 servings.

Conventional Cooking:
1. *Sauté vegetables lightly. Stir in seasoned beaten eggs. Cook over medium heat, stirring and folding as eggs cook.*
2. *Cook 15 to 20 minutes, or to desired doneness.*

RICE CHEESE CUSTARD

2 cups hot milk
1½ cups grated sharp
    cheddar cheese
1 tablespoon minced onion
2 tablespoons butter or
    margarine

½ teaspoon salt
Dash paprika
2 eggs, beaten
3 cups hot cooked rice
Broiled tomato slices;
    optional (page 163)

Warm milk in glass measure 2½ minutes in Radarange oven. Mix first 6 ingredients in 8-inch square baking dish. Cook in oven 3 minutes, stirring at 1 minute intervals. Mix a little of the hot cheese sauce into eggs; stir eggs and rice into cheese sauce. Mix well. Cook in oven 8 minutes, turning dish at 2-minute intervals a quarter turn. Cover; let stand 10 minutes before serving. To serve, cut in squares; top each square with slice of broiled tomato. Makes 6 to 8 servings.

Conventional Cooking:
1. *Make a cheese sauce with first 6 ingredients. Mix with remaining ingredients. Pour into greased baking dish.*
2. *Cover, bake in moderate oven, 375°, for about 1 hour, or until set.*

SAVORY BACON OMELET

2 tablespoons butter or margarine
½ cup thinly sliced scallions
8 medium eggs, beaten
½ pound bacon (9–10 strips), cooked and crumbled (page 75)

¼ cup whipping cream
¼ teaspoon pepper
Salt to taste
2 teaspoons prepared mustard

Heat butter in Radarange oven in 10-inch glass pie plate 30 seconds. Stir in scallions. Cook in oven 1 minute. Mix together eggs, bacon, cream, and seasonings. Pour into dish; mix with scallions. Cook 4 to 6 minutes, stirring twice from outside edge to center. Let stand 3 minutes; fold; turn onto warm platter. Makes 4 servings.

Conventional Cooking:
1. *Sauté scallions until limp; add remaining ingredients.*
2. *Cook over medium heat about 10 minutes, stirring twice from outside edge to center.*

SCRAMBLED BACON AND EGGS

1 tablespoon butter or margarine
¼ cup finely chopped green
pepper
½ can (5½ oz.) condensed
cream of chicken soup*

4 eggs, slightly beaten
Season to taste
6 slices bacon, cooked and
crumbled (page 75)

Place butter in shallow 2-quart glass baking dish. Add green pepper; cook in Radarange oven 30 seconds. Mix soup and eggs, blend well. Stir egg mixture into sautéed green pepper. Cook 4½ to 5 minutes, stirring 3 or 4 times. Season to taste. Crumble bacon on top. Makes 3 to 4 servings.

*Other cream soup flavors can be substituted—mushroom, celery, etc.

Conventional Cooking:
1. Heat butter in skillet, sauté green pepper. Combine and stir in remaining ingredients.
2. Use a fork to stir and scramble mixture over medium heat to desired doneness. Add bacon.

WELSH RAREBIT

1 cup beer or ale*	½ teaspoon dry mustard
1 tablespoon butter or margarine	1 teaspoon salt
	½ teaspoon paprika
1 pound sharp natural cheddar cheese, grated	1 teaspoon Worcestershire sauce
1 egg, beaten	Dash cayenne

Pour beer into 2-quart casserole or bowl; add butter. Cook in oven 2 minutes. Stir in cheese. Cook, covered, in Radarange oven 2 minutes. Stir. Cook in oven 1 minute. Blend egg with seasonings, stir into cheese mixture with wire whisk. Cook in oven 1 to 1½ minutes, uncovered. Stir well before serving over hot buttered toast. Makes 6 servings.

*Pink Rarebit: Substitute 1 can (10½ oz.) tomato soup for beer.

Conventional Cooking:
1. Heat beer, stir in butter and cheese. Cook over low heat until cheese melts. Beat together remaining ingredients; stir into cheese.
2. Simmer and stir over low moderate heat until smooth, blended, and hot. Takes about 15 minutes.

CHAPTER 3:

Vegetables in Variety

Vegetables need never be monotonous nor receive a "turn-down" from the family when you have a Radarange oven to speed up defrosting and cooking times, plus a dash of imagination in concocting unusual and flavorful recipes.

Consider Hot Chili-Cheese Tomatoes, Italian Eggplant, Cauliflower Piquant, Mandarin Carrots, Ratatouille, Lemon Potatoes—just a few of the delightful recipes in this chapter. You will also find a chart to guide you in defrosting frozen vegetables, and a timetable for cooking fresh vegetables "just plain." To the latter you can add your own touches in the way of seasoning with herbs and spices, a dash of onion powder, a sauce made in minutes in the Radarange oven.

No more coaxing—no more stern warning—"eat your vegetables or you can't have any dessert." Vegetables cooked in a microwave oven are always crisp—never soggy. They have an extra fresh flavor and keep their bright colors. What a grand feeling when "seconds" are called for by former vegetable haters!

Tips on cooking vegetables

Correct timing is very important when cooking vegetables in the Radarange oven.

Test vegetables frequently during cooking.

Most vegetables will cook faster and more evenly if covered. Stir vegetables midway through cooking time.

Be careful not to overcook vegetables. Vegetables cooked with microwaves will continue to cook after the Radarange oven shuts off, so allow vegetables to stand for a few minutes before serving. Remember that vegetables become dehydrated and tough when overcooked.

For frozen vegetables

Several food packaging companies now include microwave oven cooking directions on their packages. Additionally, a chart on the next pages provides guidelines for cooking nearly every variety of frozen vegetables in the Radarange oven. **Frozen vegetables in pouch packs** *are "made to order" for microwave cooking. Simply lay the pouch on a paper plate or other suitable place. Pierce a small hole in the top of the pouch. Cook for ¼ the amount of time suggested on the package (unless microwave cooking instructions are given). Turn the dish halfway through the cooking. Remove dish and pouch, open pouch and serve.*

For canned vegetables

Drain some liquid from the can, then empty the contents into a casserole. Cover. Heat 4 to 8 minutes, or until liquid boils. Stir once during heating time.

For fresh vegetables

To serve vegetables unsurpassed in bright, natural colors and delicate flavors, follow the instructions for Radarange oven cooking of fresh vegetables in the tables in this chapter.

153

FROZEN VEGETABLES	AMOUNT	CONTAINER	SPECIAL INSTRUCTIONS	COOKING TIMES
Asparagus, green spears	1 10-oz. pkg.	1 qt. glass casserole, covered	Ice side up. Separate spears after 3 min.	5–6 min.
Asparagus, green spears	2 10-oz. pkgs.	1½ qt. glass casserole, covered	Ice side up. Separate spears after 5 min.	9½–10½ min.
Broccoli	1 10-oz. pkg.	1 qt. glass casserole, covered	Ice side up. Separate pieces after 5 min.	8½–9½ min.
Broccoli	2 10-oz. pkgs.	1½ qt. glass casserole, covered	Ice side up. Separate pieces after 8 min.	16–17 min.
Beans, Green Cut Beans, Wax	1 10-oz. pkg.	1 qt. glass casserole, covered	If solid pack, place ice side up; for loose pack, add 2 tbsp. hot water. Stir after 4 min.	7½–8½ min.
Beans, Green Cut Beans, Wax	2 10-oz. pkgs.	1½ qt. glass casserole, covered	If solid pack, place ice side up; for loose pack, add 4 tbsp. hot water. Stir after 8 min.	14–15 min.
Beans, Green French Cut	1 10-oz. pkg.	1 qt. glass casserole, covered	Add 2 tbsp. hot water. Stir after 4 min.	7–8 min.
Beans, Green French Cut	2 10-oz. pkgs.	1½ qt. glass casserole, covered	Add ¼ cup hot water. Stir after 6 min.	13–14 min.
Beans, Lima Fordhook	1 10-oz. pkg.	1 qt. glass casserole, covered	Add ¼ cup hot water. Stir after 5 min.	8½–9½ min.
Beans, Lima Fordhook	2 10-oz. pkgs.	1½ qt. glass casserole, covered	Add ¼ cup hot water. Stir after 10 min.	15–16 min.
Cauliflower	1 10-oz. pkg.	1 qt. glass casserole, covered	Add 2 tbsp. hot water.	5–6 min.
Cauliflower	2 10-oz. pkgs.	1½ qt. glass casserole, covered	Add ¼ cup hot water. Stir after 4 min.	9½–10½ min.
Corn, Cut	1 10-oz. pkg.	1 qt. glass casserole, covered	Add ¼ cup hot water.	4–5 min.

FROZEN VEGETABLES	AMOUNT	CONTAINER	SPECIAL INSTRUCTIONS	COOKING TIMES
Corn, Cut	2 10-oz. pkgs.	1½ qt. glass casserole, covered	Add ¼ cup hot water. Stir after 4 min.	7½–8½ min.
Corn on Cob	1 10-oz. pkg., (2 ears)	1 qt. glass casserole, covered	Add ¼ cup hot water. Turn after 3 min.	5–6 min.
Corn on Cob	2 10-oz. pkgs., (4 ears)	1½ qt. glass casserole, covered	Add ¼ cup hot water. Turn after 5 min.	9–10 min.
Mixed Vegetables	1 10-oz. pkg.	1 qt. glass casserole, covered	Add ¼ cup hot water.	6½–7½ min.
Mixed Vegetables	2 10-oz. pkgs.	1½ qt. glass casserole, covered	Add ¼ cup hot water. Stir after 5 min.	11–12 min.
Okra	1 10-oz. pkg.	1 qt. glass casserole, covered	Add 2 tbsp. hot water.	6–7 min.
Okra	2 10-oz. pkgs.	1½ qt. glass casserole, covered	Add ¼ cup hot water. Stir after 5 min.	11–12 min.
Peas, Green	1 10-oz. pkg.	1 qt. glass casserole, covered	If solid pack, place ice side up; for loose pack, add 2 tbsp. hot water.	4½–5½ min.
Peas, Green	2 10-oz. pkgs.	1½ qt. glass casserole, covered	If solid pack, place ice side up; for loose pack, add ¼ cup hot water. Stir after 4 min.	8–9 min.
Peas & Carrots	1 10-oz. pkg.	1 qt. glass casserole, covered	If solid pack, place ice side up; for loose pack, add 2 tbsp. hot water.	5–6 min.
Peas & Carrots	2 10-oz. pkgs.	1½ qt. glass casserole, covered	If solid pack, place ice side up; for loose pack, add ¼ cup hot water. Stir after 5 min.	10–11 min.
Spinach	1 10-oz. pkg.	1 qt. glass casserole, covered	Ice side up.	4½–5½ min.
Spinach	2 10-oz. pkgs.	1½ qt. glass casserole, covered	Ice side up. Stir after 5 min.	8–9 min.

Fresh Vegetables	Amount	Container	Special Instructions	Cooking Times
Asparagus	1 lb. 2 tbsp. water	1½ qt. covered casserole	For thick spears increase water to ¼ cup and cooking time by 2–3 min.	Cook 6 min. Stir twice during this time.
Beans, Green (Pole Beans)	3 cups	1½ qt. covered casserole	Clean and cut into 1-inch pieces. Remove strings.	Cook 10–12 min. Stir every 3 min. Rest 5 min.
Beans, Green	1 lb. ¼ cup water	1½ qt. covered casserole	Wash. Drain. Trim ends, break in half.	Cook 8 min. Rest 2 min. Stir at 4.
Beans, Yellow Wax	1 lb. ¼ cup water	2 qt. covered casserole	Wash beans, cut into 1½-inch pieces.	Cook 13 min. Stir several times.
Beets	1½ lbs. ½ cup water	4 qt. covered casserole	Trim beets, leaving 1-inch of tops attached to prevent bleeding.	Cook beets covered, 15 min. Time will vary with size.
Broccoli	1½ lbs. ½ cup water	2 qt. covered casserole	Remove the large leaves and the tough part of the stalk. Cut deep gashes in bottom of stalks.	Cook 11 min. Rearrange stalks halfway through cooking.
Brussels Sprouts	1½ lbs. ½ cup water	1½ qt. covered casserole	If wilted, pull off outer leaves. Cut stems off.	Cook 8 min. Stir at 4 min. Rest 10 min., drain.
Cabbage, Red or White	1¾ lbs. (medium head) ¼ cup water	2½ qt. covered casserole	Remove outer leaves. Wash, quarter, remove core. Coarsely shred.	Cook 11 min. Stir occasionally. Drain.
Cabbage, Chinese Celery	1 lb. ¼ cup water	1½ qt. covered casserole	Coarsely shred cabbage.	Cook 8 min. or until barely tender. Drain.
Carrots	1 lb., whole ¼ cup water	1 qt. covered casserole	Clean and cut in 1-inch pieces.	Cook 8 min. Rest, covered, 5 min.
Cauliflower	1 lb., whole ¼ cup water 1 lb. flowerets ¼ cup water	2½ qt. covered casserole 1½ qt. covered casserole	Clean. Clean, cut into flowerets.	Cook 10 min. Drain and season. Cook 8 min. Drain and season.
Celery	4 cups 2 tbsp. water	1½ qt. covered casserole	Slice on diagonal 1-inch pieces.	Cook 7–9 min.

Fresh Vegetables	Amount	Container	Special Instructions	Cooking Times
Corn on the Cob	4 ears	None	See page 168.	Cook 8 min.
Eggplant	4 cups, diced ¼ cup water ½ tsp. salt	10 inch covered ceramic baking dish.	An eggplant discolors. Quickly drop pieces into cooking liquid.	Cook 5 min. Stir. Rest 5 min., covered.
Mushrooms	½ lbs. 2 tbsp. butter or margarine	1 qt. covered casserole	Wash mushrooms gently. Trim off spots and stems. Slice whole mushrooms.	Cook 4 min. Stir once.
Onions, small white	1 lb. 1 tbsp. water	1 qt. covered casserole	Cut off root end. Remove tough outer peel.	Cook 6 min. Rest, covered for 5 min.
Okra	1 lb. 2 tbsp. water 2 tbsp. butter or margarine	1½ qt. covered casserole	Cut off stems. Leave small pods whole and cut large pods into ½-inch slices.	Heat water and butter 1 min. Add okra, cook 5 min. or until tender.
Parsnips	4 medium ¼ cup water	1½ qt. covered casserole	Pare or scrub with brush. Quarter.	Cook 8-10 min.
Peas, Green	2 cups (2 lbs.) 2 tbsp. water	1 qt. covered casserole	Shell just before cooking.	Cook 6 min. Stir at 3 min.
Pea Pods (Chinese)	4 cups (4 lbs.) ¼ cup water	1½ qt. covered casserole	Shell just before cooking.	Cook 9-10 min. Stir once.
Pea Pods (Chinese)	1 lb. 2 tbsp. water	1½ qt. covered casserole	Wash and sort.	Cook 10 min. Stir twice.
Potatoes, Red Boiled	4 large (2 lbs.) ½ cup water	2 qt. covered casserole	Cut into eighths.	Cook 12-15 min. Turn dish at 6-7 min.
Potatoes, New Boiled in Jackets	6 new red potatoes about 2 inch in diameter ¼ cup water	2 qt. covered casserole	Scrub potatoes.	Cook 10 min. Turn at 5 min.

Fresh Vegetables	Amount	Container	Special Instructions	Cooking Times
Potatoes, Sweet	2 medium, 7-8 oz. each	None	Prepare as you would regular baking potatoes.	Cook 8-11 min.
	4 medium	None	As above	Cook 15-18 min.
Rutabaga	1-1¼ lbs. (3 cups, cubed) 1/3 cup water	1½ qt. covered casserole	Peel and cube.	Cook 10 min. Stir twice.
Spinach	½ lb. ¼ cup water	2 qt. covered casserole	Discard roots and tough stems. Wash in several waters.	Cook 4 min.
Squash, Acorn	1-1½ lb.	Paper plate	Pierce skin several times.	Cook 8 min. Turn at 4 min. Split, remove seeds, cook 4 min.
Squash, Butternut	1 lb.	Paper plate	Make 2 slits on opposite side of neck of squash with paring knife. Make 2 or 3 in the body of squash. Place on paper plate.	Cook 8 min. Stand 3-5 min. Scoop out of shell. Season and serve.
Squash, Summer Yellow Crookneck	5 small, about 1 lb. 2 tbsp. water	1½ qt. covered casserole	Remove stem and blossom ends. Cut squash in half lengthwise.	Cook 6½ min.
Swiss Chard	¾ lb. ¼ cup water	4 qt. ceramic Dutch oven	Discard roots and tough stems. Wash in several waters.	Cook 7 min. or until tender.
Tomatoes, Baked	2 medium (1 lb.)	Uncovered dish	Cut in half crosswise. Dot with butter.	Cook 3-4 min.
Turnips	1 bunch ¼ cup water	1½ qt. covered casserole	Wash, peel and cut into small cubes.	Cook 10 min. Stir and turn at 5 min. Drain. Season.
Zucchini	2 medium (3 cups) ¼ cup water	1 qt. covered casserole	Slice in ¼ inch rounds.	Cook 7 min. Stir once.

ASPARAGUS SEASHORE STYLE

2 packages (10 oz. each)
   asparagus pieces
¼ cup water
1 can (10½ oz.) cream of
   shrimp soup
1 package (3 oz.) cream
   cheese, softened

Dash Cayenne pepper
1 can (4½ oz.) small
   shrimp, drained
½ cup buttered crumbs
Paprika

Place asparagus and water in 2-quart glass utility dish. Cover loosely with plastic film. Cook in Radarange oven 5 minutes. Separate spears with a fork, cover and cook 4½ to 5 minutes more, drain. Blend soup, cream cheese, and pepper until smooth; stir in shrimp. Pour over asparagus. Top with buttered crumbs; sprinkle with paprika. Cook in oven, uncovered, 8 minutes, turning dish halfway around after 4 minutes. Makes 6 servings.

Conventional Cooking:
1. Cook asparagus in water to cover until tender. Drain and turn into casserole. Add remaining ingredients as directed.
2. Bake in a moderate oven, 350°, about 25 minutes.

BAKED BROCCOLI FONDUE

1⅓ cups milk
1⅓ cups soft white bread
    crumbs
½ teaspoon salt
¼ cup butter or margarine

4 eggs, separated
1½ cups well drained,
    chopped broccoli
⅔ cups grated sharp cheese

Warm milk in glass measure in Radarange oven 2 minutes. Mix together crumbs, salt, and butter with milk. Beat egg yolks. Stir milk mixture into egg yolks. Turn into 2- to 2½-quart casserole. Cook in oven 45 seconds; stir every 15 seconds. Add broccoli and cheese; mix well. Let cool slightly. Beat egg whites stiff, fold in. Cook uncovered in oven 9 minutes, turning dish a quarter turn every 3 minutes. Let stand 3 to 4 minutes before serving. Makes 6 servings.

Conventional Cooking:
1. *Prepare and combine ingredients as directed. Turn into casserole.*
2. *Cover, bake in a moderate oven, 350°, about 45 minutes.*

BAKED PEAS

2 packages (10 oz. each)
    frozen peas
¼ cup hot water
2 tablespoons butter or margarine
2 tablespoons flour
½ teaspoon salt

⅛ teaspoon pepper
Pinch celery seed
1 cup light cream
6 slices bacon, cooked and
    crumbled (page 75),
    divided

Cook peas, covered, in 1½-quart casserole with hot water in Radarange oven 8 minutes. Stir after 4 minutes. Drain.

Make medium White Sauce (page 235) with butter, flour, seasonings, and light cream.

Cook bacon until crisp: crumble. Combine cooked peas, white sauce, and half of crumbled bacon. Stir. Top with remaining bacon. Makes 6 to 8 servings.

Conventional Cooking:
1. *Cook peas. Drain. Cook bacon until crisp. Crumble. Make white sauce with rest of ingredients.*
2. *Combine peas, white sauce, and crumbled bacon. Serve.*

BAKED POTATOES

Select uniform, medium size baking potatoes, about 7 ounces each. Scrub potatoes well. Pierce each potato all the way through with a large fork. Arrange potatoes on a paper towel laid in Radarange oven. Leave about 1 inch space between potatoes and avoid placing one potato in the center surrounded by other potatoes. Bake in oven for the times indicated below; these times are approximate and will vary according to the size and variety being cooked. Turn potatoes over about midway through cooking time.

1 potato — 4–6 minutes
2 potatoes— 8–11 minutes
4 potatoes—16–19 minutes

Note: If potatoes feel slightly firm after recommended cooking time, allow a few minutes standing time. Potatoes will finish cooking on their own.

Conventional Cooking:
1. *Rub potatoes with a little fat or oil.*
2. *Bake potatoes 45 minutes to 1 hour in hot oven.*

BARBECUED CORN

6 ears corn, shucked and   Salt and pepper
    washed   Barbecue seasoning
Melted butter or margarine
    (4–5 tablespoons)

Arrange corn in shallow oblong baking pan. Melt butter in Radarange oven. Brush corn generously with butter. Sprinkle with salt, pepper, and barbecue seasoning. Cover with plastic film. Cook in oven 10 to 12 minutes, turning dish around halfway through cooking time. Let stand a few minutes before serving. Makes 3 to 4 servings.

Conventional Cooking:
1. *Place corn in baking pan, season, add water halfway up sides of dish, and cover with foil.*
2. *Cook in a moderately hot oven, 375°, about 35 minutes, or until tender.*

BEST GREEN BEANS

1 large onion, finely   ¼ teaspoon mixed herb sea-
    chopped   soning
2 tablespoons butter or   2 cans (1 lb. each) cut green
    margarine   beans, drained
1 cup dairy sour cream   ¼ cup crumbled blue cheese
1 teaspoon salt   ½ cup Buttered Bread
¼ teaspoon seasoned pep-   Crumbs (page 223)
    per

Place onion and butter in 1½-quart casserole; cook in Radarange oven 2 minutes. Stir in sour cream and seasonings. Add beans; mix well. Sprinkle with cheese and crumbs. Cover. Cook in oven 6 minutes, turning dish a quarter turn 3 times. Let stand 5 minutes before serving. Makes 8 servings.

Conventional Cooking:
1. *Sauté onion in butter. Add remaining ingredients as directed. Turn into casserole, top with cheese and crumbs.*
2. *Bake uncovered in casserole in moderate oven, 350°, 20 to 25 minutes.*

BROILED TOMATO SLICES

1 tablespoon butter or margarine
2 large firm ripe tomatoes
cut into 6 thick slices
French or Italian style bottled salad dressing

2 tablespoons Buttered
Bread Crumbs (page 223)
1 tablespoon grated Parmesan cheese

Heat Browning Skillet in Radarange oven 4½ minutes. Add butter. Dip tomato slices in dressing, place 6 slices in skillet. Cook in oven 2 minutes, turn slices over at end of 1 minute. Remove from pan, sprinkle lightly with mixed crumbs and cheese. Makes 6 slices.

Conventional Cooking:
1. *Prepare tomatoes as directed. Arrange in single layer in shallow baking dish.*
2. *Broil about 5 to 6 minutes, sprinkle with crumbs and cheese.*

BUTTERED ONIONS AND WALNUTS

3 tablespoons butter or
margarine
½ cup walnut halves

3 cups canned small white
onions, drained
Salt and pepper

Preheat large Browning Skillet in Radarange oven 2½ minutes. Add butter and walnuts. Mix well. Cook ½ minute, stirring once. Drain off fat; add onions. Mix lightly; cook 2 minutes, or long enough to heat onions. Season with salt and pepper. Makes 6 servings.

Conventional Cooking:
1. *Melt butter, sauté walnuts. Drain off most of excess fat, add onions.*
2. *Cook and stir over medium heat until heated through, about 10 minutes.*

CABBAGE CASSEROLE

1 small cabbage	Dash pepper
2 cups boiling water	½ teaspoon paprika
1 pound lamb shoulder or neck, ground (about 2 cups)	1 teablespoon instant onion
2 cups cooked brown rice	1 tablespoon lemon juice
2 tablespoons soft butter or margarine	1 teaspoon sugar
1 teaspoon salt	1 teaspoon dried mint leaves
	½ cup catchup

Core cabbage, place in 2½-quart covered casserole, add 2 cups boiling water. Cover, cook in Radarange oven 4 minutes. Drain and cool cabbage, strip off outside leaves. Line a shallow 2-quart baking dish with overlapping large leaves, reserve 4 to 5 leaves for top. Shred or finely chop remaining cabbage, mix together with remaining ingredients. Turn mixture into lined casserole; level top; cover with reserved leaves. Cover, cook in oven 12 to 14 minutes, turn dish 180° after 6 minutes. Cover, let stand 10 minutes before serving. Makes 6 servings.

Conventional Cooking:
1. *Boil cabbage with 2 cups water about 10 to 15 minutes. Prepare casserole with cabbage leaves. Mix remaining ingredients. Layer as directed above.*
2. *Bake in 350° oven about 1 hour.*

CAULIFLOWER PIQUANT

1 medium head cauliflower
3 tablespoons hot water
½ cup mayonnaise
1 teaspoon salt

1 tablespoon prepared mustard
½ cup shredded sharp cheddar cheese

Remove leaves and trim base of cauliflower; rinse. Place in 1½-quart casserole with 3 tablespoons hot water. Cover, cook in Radarange oven about 8 to 10 minutes, until tender; drain. Mix together remaining ingredients, spread over the top of the cauliflower. Cook in oven 1½ to 2 minutes, uncovered, until sauce topping bubbles and melts. Makes 5 to 6 servings.

Conventional Cooking:
1. *Trim cauliflower. Add water to cover. Cook until fork tender, about 20 minutes. Drain. Combine remaining ingredients, spread over cauliflower.*
2. *Cook in a hot oven, 400°, about 8 to 10 minutes until topping bubbles.*

CELERY CABBAGE

1 head celery (Chinese) cabbage (about 1 pound)
¼ cup water

3 to 4 tablespoons butter or margarine
Salt, pepper, paprika

Remove root ends of Chinese cabbage, and shred stalks. Place shredded cabbage and water in 1½-quart covered casserole. Cook in oven 8 minutes, or until fork tender. Stir once. Serve buttered with salt, pepper, and paprika. Makes 4 servings.

Conventional Cooking:
1. *Prepare cabbage as directed; place in saucepan with water to almost cover.*
2. *Cook over medium heat until tender, about 25 minutes. Drain, add butter and seasonings.*

165

CHINESE PEAS

1 package (7 oz.) frozen
    Chinese peas (edible
    pod peas)
1 tablespoon butter or
    margarine
½ cup chicken stock

½ cup thinly sliced water
    chestnuts
2 teaspoons cornstarch
2 tablespoons cold water
    (or chicken stock)
¼ teaspoon salt

Measure frozen peas, butter, and chicken stock into a 1-quart bowl. Cook, uncovered, in Radarange oven for 7 minutes; stir once about midway. Add chestnuts; toss with peas; push vegetables to one side of dish. Combine cornstarch with 2 tablespoons cold water or stock and add to liquid in cooking dish; stir well. Cook 3 minutes, stirring liquid at 1 minute intervals. Mix all ingredients lightly but thoroughly. Add salt to taste. Serve hot. Makes 4 servings.

Conventional Cooking:
1. Empty contents of package into ½ cup chicken stock, add ½ teaspoon salt and butter, boil 2 minutes with frequent stirring. Add chestnuts; toss with peas.
2. Add thickening, cook over low heat, stirring to prevent lumps.

COLCANNON

1 cup chopped onion
¼ cup butter or margarine,
   divided
2 cups seasoned mashed
   potato
1 cup chopped cooked cab-
   bage

Salt and pepper
½ cup Buttered Bread
   Crumbs (page 223)
½ cup grated sharp
   cheese

Place onion and 2 tablespoons butter in shallow baking dish. Cook in Radarange oven 4 minutes; stir 2 or 3 times. Add potato and cabbage, mix well. Cover; cook in oven 1½ minutes. Sprinkle with salt, pepper, and crumbs; dot with remaining butter; top with cheese. Cook in oven 2 minutes until cheese melts. Makes 4 servings.

Conventional Cooking:
1. *Sauté onion in hot butter. Stir in potato and cabbage. Turn into casserole (or leave in pan if desired). Top with crumbs and cheese.*
2. *Bake in moderate oven, 350°, about 25 to 30 minutes.*

COMPANY BROCCOLI

2 tablespoons butter
2 tablespoons flour
½ teaspoon salt
1 cup milk
1 package (3 oz.) cream
   cheese at room tem-
   perature

½ cup shredded Swiss
   cheese
2 packages (10 oz. each)
   frozen chopped broccoli
⅓ cup Buttered Bread
   Crumbs (page 223)

Make White Cheese Sauce in 1-quart casserole (see page 235) using first six ingredients. Cook frozen broccoli in 1½- to 2-quart casserole, ice side up, covered, 8 minutes. Separate pieces with a fork, drain. Add White Cheese Sauce to broccoli, stir well. Top with buttered crumbs. Cook 3 minutes, uncovered; turn dish completely around, cook 3 minutes more. Makes 8 servings.

Conventional Cooking:
1. *In saucepan cook broccoli in water to cover until tender. Drain; turn into casserole. Make sauce with other ingredients; stir into broccoli. Top with crumbs.*
2. *Bake in a moderate oven, 350°, about 35 to 40 minutes.*

CORN-ON-THE-COB

Pull off outer husks, leaving only an inner husk on four ears of fresh sweet corn. Carefully pull back inner husks and remove silk. Brush ears with melted butter and season with salt if you wish. Replace husks and fasten with string or rubber band on tip of each ear. Lay four ears in a glass utility dish. Cook 4 minutes in Radarange oven. Roll ears half way over and turn dish one-half turn. Cook 4 minutes longer. Remove string and serve. Allow husks to remain around the ear until ready to eat as this will maintain the heat. Turn back the husks and use as a handle for eating the corn.

CORN PUDDING

2 tablespoons butter or margarine
1 tablespoon flour
1 teaspoon salt
1 teaspoon sugar
Pepper and paprika to taste
1 can (8 oz.) whole kernel corn, drained

1 can (1 lb.) cream style corn
4 medium eggs, separated
¾ cup dairy sour cream
Bread crumbs

Add butter to 1½- to 2-quart casserole, heat in Radarange oven 1 minute. Mix flour, seasonings, and two kinds of corn; blend in beaten egg yolk and sour cream. Mix thoroughly. Fold in stiffly beaten egg whites. Pour corn mixture into casserole; sprinkle with fine bread crumbs. Cook in oven 5 minutes; turn dish one quarter turn, cook 2 minutes more; turn one quarter turn again. Cook corn pudding 3 more minutes. Let stand a few minutes before serving. Makes 5 to 6 servings.

Conventional Cooking:
1. *Melt butter, proceed as above. Fold in stiffly beaten egg whites. Turn mixture into greased baking dish.*
2. *Bake in slow moderate oven, 325°, about 40 to 50 minutes, until puffed and set.*

CREAMED ONIONS

1 pound small white onions, peeled
1 tablespoon water
2 tablespoons butter or margarine

2 tablespoons flour
½ teaspoon salt
1 cup milk
Dash nutmeg

Place onions and water in a 1- to 1½-quart casserole. Cook in Radarange oven 6 minutes. Let stand 5 minutes; drain. Melt butter in 1-quart glass casserole or bowl in oven for 30 seconds. Stir in flour and salt; blend to a smooth paste. Add milk gradually, stirring constantly. Cook, uncovered, in oven for 1 minute. Stir well. Cook 1½ to 2 minutes longer, stirring every 30 seconds. Pour White Sauce over onions; add a few dashes of nutmeg. Makes 4 servings.

Conventional Cooking:
1. *Cook peeled onions in saucepan, with water to cover, until onions are tender, about 15 minutes. Prepare White Sauce as directed. Cook over medium heat until thickened.*
2. *Drain onions, add sauce.*

CREAMY GREEN BEANS AND MUSHROOMS

1 pound fresh green beans
¼ cup water
1 can (3 oz.) sliced mushrooms, drained
1 cup dairy sour cream

1 tablespoon flour
1 tablespoon brown sugar
½ teaspoon salt
Dash pepper

Rinse and drain beans. Trim ends, snap in two. Place in 1½-quart covered glass casserole with water. Cook in Radarange oven 8 minutes, let stand 2 minutes, drain. Stir in mushrooms. Mix remaining ingredients, stir into beans and mushrooms. Cover. Cook in oven 3 to 4 minutes. Stir and let stand, covered, 5 minutes before serving. Makes 5 to 6 servings.

Conventional Cooking:
1. *Prepare beans, add hot water to cover. Cook until tender; drain. Add remaining ingredients.*
2. *Cook over medium heat, stirring several times, until heated through and bubbling, about 10 to 12 minutes.*

DELICIOUS SWISS CHARD

1 pound fresh Swiss chard	2 tablespoons lemon juice
1 teaspoon salt	¼ teaspoon seasoned
Pinch instant minced garlic	pepper
¼ cup water	2 to 3 tablespoons grated
3 tablespoons olive oil	Parmesan cheese

Discard roots, tough stems, and wilted leaves; wash chard, chop stems. Place salt and water in bottom of 1½-quart casserole; add wet chard on top. Sprinkle with garlic. Cover; cook in Radarange oven 5 minutes until crisply tender, stirring twice. Mix together remaining ingredients; pour over chard. Use 2 sharp knives to cut through chard several times. Toss to mix. Cook in oven 2 minutes. Toss again before serving. Makes 4 servings.

Conventional Cooking:
1. *Combine Swiss chard with next 3 ingredients. Cook in heavy 1½-quart covered saucepan over medium heat, about 15 minutes.*
2. *Add remaining ingredients, cook 5 minutes longer.*

EGGPLANT PARMIGIANA

¼ cup butter or margarine,
divided
1 medium eggplant
4 large tomatoes, peeled
and sliced

½ pound mozzarella
cheese, sliced
½ cup grated Parmesan
cheese

Melt butter in small bowl in Radarange oven 30 seconds.
Cut eggplant in ½-inch slices. Sprinkle with salt; stack with
heavy weight on top. Let stand 2 hours; rinse off salt, drain,
dry on paper towels. Put 2 tablespoons melted butter in
8"x8"-square baking dish; arrange a layer of eggplant slices,
a layer of tomato slices, a layer of mozzarella, and a layer
of grated Parmesan. Add rest of butter, repeat layers, cover
with plastic film wrap. Cook in oven 9 minutes, turning dish
a quarter turn every 3 minutes. Let stand a few minutes
before serving. Cut into squares. Makes 4 servings.

Conventional Cooking:
1. Sauté eggplant slices in hot butter to brown on both sides.
   Layer ingredients, as directed, in casserole.
2. Bake in a moderate oven, 350°, about 45 to 50 minutes.

HOLIDAY SQUASH

2 acorn squash (about 14–
16 ounces each)
1 cup canned whole cran-
berry sauce
¼ cup canned crushed
pineapple

¼ cup brown sugar
3 tablespoons soft butter or
margarine
½ teaspoon cinnamon
⅛ teaspoon nutmeg

Pierce whole acorn squash with a fork in several places.
Cook whole in Radarange oven 8 minutes, turn over after 4
minutes cooking. Cut in half, discard seeds and place cut
sides up in 2-quart shallow baking dish. Mix together re-

maining ingredients, fill squash halves with mixture. Cover with plastic film wrap, cook in oven 8 minutes, turn dish halfway through cooking time. Makes 4 servings.

Conventional Cooking:
1. *Place squash, cut side down in shallow baking dish. Add ½ cup hot water. Cook in moderate oven, 375°, about 25 minutes.*
2. *Turn squash halves over, fill with combined remaining ingredients. Cover with foil, cook another 20 or 30 minutes until very tender.*

HOT CHILI-CHEESE TOMATOES

10 medium size firm ripe
  tomatoes, peeled
1 cup dairy sour cream
½ teaspoon salt
¼ teaspoon pepper
1 teaspoon sugar
2 tablespoons chopped
  green onion

1 tablespoon flour
2 tablespoons chopped
  canned green chilies
1 cup shredded Longhorn
  or Monterey Jack cheese

Cut tomatoes in half; squeeze each gently to drain off some of the excess liquid and seeds. Arrange 5 tomatoes (10 halves) cut side up in 2-quart shallow baking pan. Thoroughly blend sour cream with seasonings, flour, and chopped chilies. Spoon 1 teaspoon mixture over each tomato. Sprinkle ½ cup cheese over all. Cook uncovered in oven for 4 minutes, turning dish after 2 minutes. Repeat procedure with remaining tomatoes. Makes 10 servings.

Conventional Cooking:
1. *Prepare ingredients as directed. Arrange tomatoes in baking dish. Top with sour cream mixture and cheese.*
2. *Bake in a moderate oven, 350°, about 18 to 20 minutes.*

ITALIAN EGGPLANT

1 small eggplant (about 1
   pound)
¼ cup chopped onion
½ cup brown sugar
2 slices dry bread,
   crumbled

1 can (1 lb.) whole
   tomatoes
½ cup cubed American
   cheese

Wash and pare eggplant. Cut into 1-inch cubes. Parboil in Radarange oven with ¼ cup water in 1½-quart covered glass casserole for 5 minutes. Drain water from eggplant. Add remaining ingredients; mix well. Cook 5 minutes. Makes 6 servings.

Conventional Cooking:

1. Parboil eggplant in water to cover. Drain; turn into casserole and stir in remaining ingredients.
2. Bake covered in a moderate oven, 350°, for about 45 minutes.

LEMON POTATOES

3 large potatoes, peeled
   and quartered (about 1½
   pounds)
Oil
2 teaspoons butter or
   margarine
2 teaspoons fresh lemon
   juice

2 teaspoons fresh lemon
   peel, grated
3 tablespoons Parmesan
   cheese, grated
¼ teaspoon paprika

Place cut potatoes in oiled 8-inch-square baking dish. Melt butter in Radarange oven 30 seconds. Add lemon juice. Spread over potatoes. Mix peel, cheese, and paprika. Sprinkle over potatoes. Cover, cook in oven 12 minutes, turning dish one quarter turn every 4 minutes. Allow to stand, covered, a few minutes before serving. Makes 4 servings.

Conventional Cooking:
1. Boil potatoes in water to cover, until just tender. Drain. Add remaining ingredients.
2. Cover, cook over moderate heat. Shake pan to prevent sticking. Cook long enough (about 5 minutes) to dry potatoes and blend flavors.

MANDARIN CARROTS

4 cups carrots, cut in 2-inch strips

2 tablespoons butter or margarine

1 can or jar (11 oz.) mandarin orange sections, drained

⅛ teaspoon ginger

½ teaspoon salt

Cook carrots and butter in 1½-quart covered casserole in Radarange oven 12 minutes. Stir at 2½ minute intervals. Add mandarin oranges, ginger, and salt; cook covered 2 minutes. Let stand 2 to 3 minutes before serving. Makes 6 servings.

Conventional Cooking:
1. Cook carrots until tender in water to cover, about 15 to 18 minutes. Drain. Stir in remaining ingredients.
2. Cover, simmer until heated through.

NEW POTATOES AND PEAS IN CREAM

1 pound small new potatoes

1 package frozen green peas, thawed

2 tablespoons butter

1 tablespoon flour

½ teaspoon salt

⅛ teaspoon pepper

½ cup light cream

1 small onion, finely chopped

To thaw frozen peas, heat, covered, in Radarange oven in 2½-quart casserole 2 minutes. Stir after one minute. Scrub potatoes; cut off a band of skin around middle of each. Pierce through once or twice with a fork. Put potatoes in a medium cooking bag. Fold open end of bag under potatoes loosely. Cook 8 minutes; turn bag over after 4 minutes of cooking. Remove potatoes from oven. Melt butter in small bowl in oven 30 seconds. Stir in flour, salt, and pepper. Add light cream gradually, stirring constantly. Cook 1 minute, stir; cook 30 seconds more. Pour sauce over peas, add onions, stir well. Add cooked potatoes from bag. Stir to coat all. Cook 3 minutes in oven. Makes 4 servings.

Conventional Cooking:
1. *Cook potatoes, covered, in boiling water to cover until tender. Drain.*
2. *In large saucepan, make cream sauce as directed, add thawed peas and chopped onions, cook 5 minutes. Add cooked potatoes.*

OKRA

1 pound fresh okra	2 tablespoons butter or
2 tablespoons water	margarine
	Salt and pepper

Wash and sort okra. Leave small pods whole; cut large pods into 1-inch pieces. Heat water and butter in 1½-quart covered glass casserole in Radarange oven 1 minute. Add okra; cover. Cook in oven 5 minutes or until tender. Season to taste with salt and pepper. Makes 4 servings.

Conventional Cooking:
1. *Prepare okra as directed. In saucepan with water to barely cover, cook over moderate heat 15 to 20 minutes until tender.*
2. *Drain, stir in butter, and season to taste.*

ORANGE BEETS

1 can (1 lb.) sliced beets,
    drained
1½ tablespoons soft butter
    or margarine
2 tablespoons cornstarch
2 tablespoons fresh lemon
    juice

1 cup orange juice
2 tablespoons sugar
¼ teaspoon salt
Pinch pepper

Turn beets into 1½-quart casserole. Mix remaining ingredients together in a bowl or 2-cup measure. Cook in Radarange oven 2 to 2½ minutes, stirring once until thickened. Add sauce to beets, mix well. Cover; cook in oven 1½ minutes. Makes 6 servings.

Conventional Cooking:
1. Heat orange juice, sugar, salt, and pepper in saucepan to a simmer over medium heat. Stir in cornstarch dissolved in lemon juice. Stir in butter. Cook and stir over low heat until thickened.
2. Stir in beets. Cook over low heat, stirring carefully, until heated through, about 5 minutes.

PEAS AND LETTUCE MEDLEY

1½ pounds fresh peas,
    shelled (2 cups)
¼ small head iceberg let-
    tuce, rinsed and coarsely
    chopped

¼ cup sliced green onions
    (scallions)
½ teaspoon sugar
¾ teaspoon salt
Butter

Place peas, wet lettuce, onions, and sugar in 1½-quart covered glass casserole. Cook in Radarange oven 3 minutes; stir, cook 3 to 4 minutes until tender. Stir in salt and butter to taste. Let stand, covered, a few minutes before serving. Makes 4 to 6 servings.

Conventional Cooking:
1. *Combine ingredients in saucepan with 3 or 4 tablespoons water.*
2. *Cover, cook until peas are tender (about 15 minutes).*

POTATO AND CARROT KUGEL

2 cups grated raw potato (about 4 medium)	¼ teaspoon pepper
¼ cup grated onion	½ cup all-purpose flour
1 cup grated raw carrot	3 tablespoons vegetable oil
¾ teaspoon salt	2 medium eggs, beaten

Combine all ingredients except eggs. Stir until well blended. Blend in eggs; mix well. Turn into 8-inch-square baking dish sprayed with vegetable oil coating. Cover, cook in Radarange oven 10 to 11 minutes, turn dish a quarter turn every 3½ minutes. Wooden pick inserted in center comes out clean when kugel is done. Let stand 5 minutes. Serve hot, cut in squares. Makes 6 servings.

Conventional Cooking:
1. *Prepare and mix ingredients as directed. Turn into greased pan.*
2. *Bake in a moderate oven, 350°, about 45 minutes or until set.*

POTATO CHEESE DELIGHT

1 package (2 lbs.) frozen
shredded hash brown
potatoes
2 cups (8 oz.) sharp cheddar cheese, grated
2 tablespoons flour
½ cup green onions (scal-
lions), chopped

½ medium green pepper,
chopped
2 teaspoons salt
¼ teaspoon pepper
1 pint whipping cream or
half and half

Defrost frozen potatoes in Radarange oven in 2-quart
covered glass casserole 7 minutes; stir after 3½ minutes.
Add remaining ingredients. Stir well. Bake, covered, 10
minutes or until cheese is completely melted. Stir after 5
minutes cooking time. Makes 6 to 8 servings.

Conventional Cooking:
1. *Grease a 2-quart casserole; add frozen hash browns.
   Cover, and cook in oven at 325°, till defrosted, about 15
   minutes.*
2. *Combine remaining ingredients with hash browns. Cover
   and return to oven. Cook another 15 to 20 minutes. Uncover last 5 minutes of baking time to brown top.*

QUEEN'S SUCCOTASH

1 package (10 oz.) frozen
succotash
1 package (10 oz.) frozen
tiny peas
½ cup milk

Pinch basil
2 tablespoons butter or
margarine
Salt and pepper

Combine all ingredients (except salt and pepper) in a 2-
quart covered casserole. Cook in Radarange oven 7 minutes;
stir after 4 minutes. Stir, cook 6 to 7 minutes more, stirring

178

halfway through cooking time. Salt and pepper to taste. Let stand, covered, a few minutes before serving. Makes 6 servings.

Conventional Cooking:
1. *Combine ingredients in a good sized saucepan.*
2. *Heat and stir over medium heat about 20 minutes.*

RATATOUILLE

½ cup thinly sliced onion
1 clove garlic, minced
1½ cups peeled diced eggplant
3 tablespoons olive oil
1 teaspoon salt
Dash pepper

¼ teaspoon Italian seasoning
1 can (1 lb.) stewed tomatoes
1 medium green pepper, cut in ½-inch strips
1½ cups zucchini, sliced

Mix together onion, garlic, eggplant, and olive oil in 2-quart covered casserole. Cook in Radarange oven 5 minutes. Add seasonings to tomatoes. Layer green peppers and zucchini over first mixture, add tomatoes. Cook, covered, in oven 8 to 10 minutes. Let stand covered 5 minutes before serving. Makes 4 to 6 servings.

Conventional Cooking:
1. *Sauté onions, garlic, and eggplant in oil. Arrange vegetables in layers in casserole.*
2. *Cover, bake in a moderate oven, 350°, 45 to 50 minutes.*

RUTABAGA PUFF

¼ cup instant minced
   onion
2 tablespoons butter or
   margarine
1½ cups hot mashed
   potatoes

1½ cups hot mashed ruta-
   bagas or turnips
1 teaspoon salt
⅛ teaspoon pepper
1 medium egg, beaten

Sauté onions and butter in small bowl in Radarange oven 2 minutes. Combine all ingredients in 1-quart casserole. Cook in oven 8 minutes, turning every 2 minutes. Makes 4 servings.

Conventional Cooking:
1. *Prepare and mix ingredients as directed. Turn into casserole.*
2. *Bake in a moderate oven, 375°, about 35 to 40 minutes.*

SAUTÉED ONIONS

1 tablespoon margarine or
   butter

1 cup chopped raw onions

Heat margarine or butter in Browning Skillet 30 to 40 seconds. Remove skillet from Radarange oven. Stir in chopped onions. Return skillet to oven. Cook, uncovered, 2½ to 3 minutes, stirring once. Makes 2 to 3 servings.

Conventional Cooking:
1. *Melt butter in pan. Stir in onions.*
2. *Cook and stir over medium-high heat, till onions are soft and yellow.*

SCALLOPED CORN

3 tablespoons butter or
  margarine
2 eggs, beaten
1 cup milk
⅔ cup coarsely crushed
  cracker crumbs
1 can (1 lb.) whole kernel
  corn, drained

1 tablespoon onion, minced
½ teaspoon salt
⅛ teaspoon pepper
1 tablespoon sugar
Dash Worcestershire sauce
Paprika

Melt butter in 1½-quart casserole in Radarange oven 45 seconds. Thoroughly mix together and add eggs, milk, and cracker crumbs. Add remaining ingredients (except paprika). Mix well. Bake 5 minutes, stir after 2½ minutes. Let stand 5 minutes. Sprinkle with paprika. Makes 4 servings.

Conventional Cooking:
1. Combine ingredients as directed.
2. Bake in greased casserole for 35 minutes at 350°.

SCALLOPED CORN AND OYSTERS

25 soda crackers, crumbled,
  divided
2 tablespoons melted butter
1 can (1 lb.) whole kernel
  corn, drained
1 can (1 lb.) cream style
  corn
1 can (10½ oz.) condensed
  oyster stew

1 cup fresh or canned
  oysters, drained
¼ cup onion, finely
  chopped
1 teaspoon salt
¼ teaspoon pepper
Paprika

Measure ¼ cup cracker crumbs. Mix with butter, set aside. Mix together remaining ingredients (except paprika) in 2½-quart casserole, cook uncovered in Radarange oven 7 minutes. Stir, sprinkle with remaining cracker crumbs and add dash of paprika. Cook in oven for 8 minutes. Let stand 4 to 5 minutes before serving. Makes 8 to 10 servings.

Conventional Cooking:
1. *Reserve ¼ cup crumbs and butter for topping. Combine remaining ingredients in casserole. Top with buttered crumbs and paprika.*
2. *Bake in a moderate oven, 350°, 40 to 50 minutes.*

SHERRIED ONIONS

2 cans (1 lb. each) small cooked onions, drained
½ cup light cream
⅓ cup dry sherry
½ teaspoon salt
⅛ teaspoon pepper
3 tablespoons butter or margarine
⅓ cup sharp cheddar cheese, shredded

Place onions in 1½-quart shallow baking dish. Mix cream, sherry, and seasonings; pour over onions. Dot with butter, sprinkle with cheese. Cover; cook in Radarange oven 4 minutes; stir, cook 1 to 2 minutes more. Stir, cover, let stand few minutes before serving. Makes 5 to 6 servings.

Conventional Cooking:
1. *Pour drained onions into casserole. Add remaining ingredients as directed.*
2. *Bake in a moderate oven, 350°, about 20 minutes.*

SHERRIED SWEETS

6 medium size sweet potatoes
4 tablespoons butter or margarine
½ cup brown sugar
⅔ cup orange juice
½ teaspoon grated orange peel
⅓ cup sherry
1 cup pecans, coarsely chopped

Rinse and dry potatoes, pierce each one several times with a fork. Place potatoes in a cooking bag with open end folded under, or on a layer of paper towels, in the Radarange oven. Cook 10 to 12 minutes, depending on the size of the potatoes. Turn them over halfway through cooking time. Cook until they are firm but almost tender. Peel and cut in 1-inch-thick slices.

Melt butter in 10-inch ceramic skillet in oven 45 seconds. Add potato slices. Cook 1 minute; stir to coat; cook 1 minute more. Mix together remaining ingredients; pour over slices. Mix gently so slices are coated but unbroken. Cover, cook in oven 10 minutes, turn dish halfway around at end of 5 minutes. Makes 4 to 6 servings.

Conventional Cooking:
1. *Boil potatoes in water to cover over medium heat until almost tender. Peel and slice. Melt butter in fry pan, lightly sauté slices. Mix and add remaining ingredients. Stir gently to coat potato slices.*
2. *Cover, bake in a moderate oven (350°) about 40 minutes, turning potato slices several times.*

STEWED TOMATOES

2 cups boiling water
3 medium size tomatoes
1 tablespoon onion, minced
2 teaspoons sugar
1 teaspoon salt

⅛ teaspoon pepper
2 tablespoons butter or margarine
½ cup soft bread cubes

Pour boiling water over tomatoes to loosen skins. Drain. Peel tomatoes, cut in fourths. Mix together tomatoes, onion, seasonings and butter in a 1½-quart casserole. Cook 3 minutes in Radarange oven. Stir in bread cubes. Cook 2 to 3 minutes. Makes 4 to 6 servings.

Conventional Cooking:
1. *Peel and quarter tomatoes. Combine with remaining ingredients in casserole.*
2. *Bake in a moderate oven, 350°, about 35 minutes.*

SWEET AND SOUR RED CABBAGE

1 medium size red cabbage,
  shredded, (about 4–5
  cups)
2 tart apples, peeled and
  chopped
3 tablespoons butter

½ cup cider vinegar
1 cup boiling water
½ teaspoon salt
3 tablespoons sugar
1 2-inch piece stick
  cinnamon

Combine ingredients in 2½ -quart covered casserole. Cover.
Cook in Radarange oven 10 to 12 minutes, stirring twice.
Makes 6 servings.

Conventional Cooking:
1. *Prepare ingredients and combine in large saucepan, adding
   additional water if necessary.*
2. *Cook over medium heat about 35 to 40 minutes, until
   cabbage is limp and liquid reduced.*

SWISS BROCCOLI CUSTARD

2 packages (10 oz. each)
  chopped broccoli,*
  thawed and well drained
1 cup half and half
4 medium eggs, beaten
1½ cups Swiss cheese,
  shredded

¼ cup packaged biscuit
  mix
½ teaspoon onion salt
Pepper and paprika to taste
2 tablespoons butter or
  margarine

Thaw frozen broccoli in 2-quart covered dish, in Radarange oven for 6 minutes. Press broccoli in a colander or
strainer to remove all liquid. Chop broccoli fine, mix with
cream and eggs. Dredge cheese with biscuit mix and seasonings. Stir into broccoli mixture. Heat butter in 10-inch
ceramic skillet or 10- to 11-inch glass pie plate in oven for
45 seconds. Spread over bottom and sides of dish. Pour

broccoli mixture into dish. Cook in oven 10 minutes. Stir from outside edge into center at end of 5 minutes. Let stand, covered, 10 minutes. Cut in wedges to serve. Garnish with bacon curls if desired. Makes 6 servings.

*Spinach or green beans may be substituted to make an equally enticing Swiss Custard.

Conventional Cooking:
1. *Prepare and mix ingredients as directed. Turn into a well-buttered shallow skillet or large pie pan.*
2. *Bake in a moderate oven, 350°, about 45 minutes or until set.*

TOLL HOUSE BAKED BEANS

2 cans (1 lb. 2 oz. each)
  New England-style baked
  beans
¼ pound sliced bacon,
  cooked and crumbled
  (page 75)
2 tablespoons dark
  molasses

1 tablespoon sugar
2 teaspoons dry mustard
1 medium onion, minced
1 can (1 lb.) solid pack
  tomatoes, drained

Turn beans into 2-quart casserole or bean pot. Mix together remaining ingredients, breaking up tomatoes. Pour over beans; mix well. Cover. Cook in Radarange oven 10 minutes, stirring twice. Let stand 10 minutes before serving. Makes 6 to 8 servings.

Conventional Cooking:
1. *Prepare as above.*
2. *Bake, covered, in 325° oven about 1 hour 10 minutes.*

VEGETABLE MELANGE

3 tablespoons butter or
 margarine
1 large onion, chopped
1 garlic clove, minced
1 medium size cauliflower,
 broken into small
 flowerets
¼ cup water or bouillon

¼ cup parsley
2 teaspoons salt
¼ teaspoon pepper
¼ teaspoon poultry
 seasoning
2 zucchini, cubed
3 large tomatoes, diced

Mix together butter and next 5 ingredients in 2-quart covered casserole. Cook in Radarange oven 5 minutes, stir. Add seasonings and zucchini. Cook 5 minutes more, stir in tomatoes, cook 2 minutes more. Let stand covered a few minutes before serving.

Conventional Cooking:
1. Heat butter in large fry pan, sauté onion, garlic, and parsley. Combine with remaining ingredients in casserole.
2. Cover, bake in a moderate oven, 375°, about 45 minutes.

VEGETABLE SPECIAL

1 package (10 oz.) frozen
 cut green beans
1 package (10 oz.) frozen
 carrot crinkles

1 package (6 oz.) garlic
 pasteurized process
 cheese, diced
1 cup canned french fried
 onion rings

Cook beans and carrots in covered 1½-quart casserole in oven 10 minutes. Stir after 5 minutes. Add cheese; cook 3 minutes until melted. Stir. Add onion rings. Cook 1½ to 2 minutes. Makes 4 to 6 servings.

Conventional Cooking:
1. Cook frozen vegetables as directed on package. Drain, turn into casserole. Add remaining ingredients.
2. Cover, bake in a moderate oven, 350°, about 35 to 40 minutes.

ZUCCHINI CASSEROLE

3 slices bacon, cooked and
  crumbled (page 75)
4 cups thinly sliced zuc-
  chini (about 3 medium)
¼ cup hot water
1 egg

½ cup dairy sour cream
1 tablespoon flour
¾ cup shredded sharp
  cheese
¼ cup Buttered Bread
  Crumbs (page 223)

Cook bacon between layers of paper toweling in Radarange oven 3 minutes. Set aside to cool. Put rinsed zucchini in 1½-quart casserole with water. Cover; cook in oven 7 minutes, drain. Mix egg, cream, flour, and cheese. Stir into zucchini. Cook 3 minutes; stir. Crumble bacon and add to bread crumbs; sprinkle on vegetable. Cook 2 minutes more. Makes 5 to 6 servings.

Conventional Cooking:
1. Cook zucchini in water to cover until almost tender. Drain. Turn into casserole. Gently stir in cream and cheese mixture. Sprinkle with bacon and crumbs.
2. Bake in moderate oven, 350°, 30 to 35 minutes.

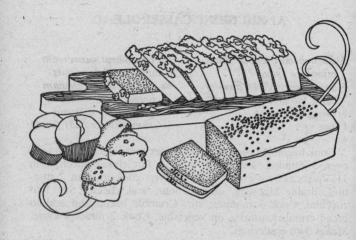

CHAPTER 4:

New-Style Baking

Breads and cakes bake beautifully to a flavorful, perfectly textured treat in the Radarange oven. For the greatest eye appeal, choose recipes for bread or unfrosted cakes that are dark in color, like chocolate, spice, gingerbread, or dark fruit cake. The same thing holds true for quick breads, muffins, bar cookies, and so on. We have chosen the following recipes with this in mind, and we are sure you will be happy with them.

APPLE NUT HEALTH BREAD

1½ cups all-purpose flour, sifted
2 teaspoons baking powder
½ teaspoon baking soda
1 teaspoon salt
1 teaspoon cinnamon
¼ teaspoon nutmeg
⅛ teaspoon allspice
1 cup ready-to-serve wheat cereal flakes, crushed

½ cup wheat germ
1 cup chopped walnuts
¾ cup apple (1 medium apple, cored), chopped
1 egg, slightly beaten
¾ cup brown sugar, firmly packed
1½ cups buttermilk
2 tablespoons vegetable oil

Mix and sift dry ingredients and spices. Stir in cereal flakes, wheat germ, walnuts, and apple. Mix together egg, brown sugar, buttermilk, and oil; add to dry mixture. Mix to moisten all dry ingredients very well. Do not beat. Turn into well-greased or sprayed glass loaf pan (9"x5"x3"). Cover with plastic wrap. Cook in Radarange oven 9 minutes, turning pan every 3 minutes a quarter turn. Let stand 10 minutes in pan. Turn out and cool on rack. Makes 1 loaf.

Conventional Cooking:
1. Prepare batter as directed. Turn into greased loaf pan.
2. Bake in moderate oven, 350°, about 1 hour or until bread tests done.

BISCUIT BREAKFAST RING

⅓ cup brown sugar
3 tablespoons butter or margarine
1 tablespoon water

⅓ cup chopped nuts
1 package (10) refrigerator biscuits

Mix together sugar, butter, and water in 1½-quart round baking dish or ceramic ring mold. Cook in Radarange oven, uncovered, 1 minute; stir until butter melts. Stir in nuts. Cut each biscuit into fourths; add to sugar mixture. Stir to coat each piece. If using a round baking dish, set a custard cup or glass in center. Cook, uncovered, 3 minutes to 3 minutes, 15 seconds, giving dish a quarter turn every 30 seconds. Remove from oven. Let stand 2 minutes. Invert on platter. Serve immediately. Makes 4 to 5 servings.

Conventional Cooking:
1. *Combine and heat first 3 ingredients over medium heat. Stir in nuts and biscuits as directed. Turn into ring mold.*
2. *Bake in hot oven, 400°, about 15 minutes. Serve warm.*

CAMDEN ELECTION DAY CAKE

1 package active dry yeast
¼ cup warm water (105°–115°)
1 teaspoon sugar
¾ cup milk, scalded
2½ cups all-purpose flour, divided
½ cup butter or margarine
¾ cup brown sugar, firmly packed

2 eggs
½ teaspoon salt
1 teaspoon cinnamon
¼ teaspoon nutmeg
⅛ teaspoon each cloves and mace
¾ cup seedless raisins, chopped
¼ cup citron, chopped

Dissolve yeast in warm water; stir in 1 teaspoon sugar. Stir in cooled milk. Add about ¾ cup flour, mix well; cover. Let rise in warm place (85°) until light and bubbly, about 40 minutes. Cream butter, beat in brown sugar gradually. Add eggs, one at a time, beating well after each addition. Add to yeast mixture. Mix and sift remaining flour, salt, and spices; stir in. Batter will be stiff. Beat until smooth. Mix in raisins and citron. Turn into greased and sprayed 10-inch china or glass bundt pan. Cover. Let rise in warm place (85°) 1½ hours. Cover with wax paper, cook in oven 9 to 10 minutes. Turn pan a quarter turn at 3-minute intervals.

Let stand 10 minutes before turning out of pan. Cool before frosting with a thin lemon glaze. Makes 1 large cake.

Lemon Glaze:

1. Blend 1¼ cups sifted confectioners' sugar, 2 tablespoons lemon juice, 1 teaspoon water, and 1 tablespoon grated lemon rind.
2. Pour over top of cake to glaze.

Conventional Cooking:
1. *Prepare cake as directed.*
2. *Bake in preheated 350° oven about 1 hour.*

CHOCOLATE APPLESAUCE NUT CAKE

¾ cup butter or margarine
1½ cups sugar
3 eggs
3 squares (1 oz. each) unsweetened chocolate, melted
¾ cup broken walnuts
2½ cups cake flour, sifted

2¼ teaspoons baking powder
¾ teaspoon baking soda
¾ teaspoon salt
1½ cups canned applesauce (15 oz. jar)
3 teaspoons vanilla
Topping*

Cream butter until light and fluffy. Cream in sugar. Add egg 1 at a time, beating well after each addition. Blend in chocolate. Stir in nuts. Mix and sift dry ingredients. Stir in alternately with applesauce. Stir in vanilla. Spoon batter into greased and floured 10-inch ceramic bundt pan. Cook in Radarange oven 11 to 12 minutes, or until wooden pick inserted near center tube comes out clean. Turn dish a quarter turn every 2 minutes of baking time. Let stand in dish 15 minutes; invert onto cake plate. Makes 1 large cake.

*Topping:

¼ cup sugar
1 tablespoon flour
1 tablespoon milk

3 tablespoons butter or margarine
½ teaspoon vanilla
⅓ cup walnuts, chopped

Combine first 5 ingredients in 2 cup measure. Cook in Radarange oven 1 minute, stirring smooth. Spoon topping mixture over cake, sprinkle with nuts.

Conventional Cooking:
1. *Mix ingredients as directed, spoon into greased and floured bundt pan.*
2. *Bake in preheated 350° oven, about 1 hour.*

COCOA CUPCAKES

½ cup butter or margarine	1½ teaspoons baking
1½ cups sugar	powder
3 eggs	½ teaspoon salt
¾ cup breakfast cocoa	1 teaspoon vanilla
(not instant)	⅔ cup milk
1½ cups all-purpose flour	1 cup cream, whipped

Cream butter; beat in sugar gradually until light and fluffy. Beat in eggs, one at a time. Mix and sift dry ingredients. Stir vanilla into milk. Add dry mixture to butter mixture, alternately, with milk. Place paper baking cups in custard cups. Fill ⅔ full with batter. Arrange 6 cupcakes in a circle in Radarange oven. Cook 3 to 3½ minutes. Repeat with remaining batter. Remove from custard cups to cooling rack immediately. Frost with whipped cream when cold. Makes about 1½ dozen cupcakes.

Conventional Cooking:
1. *Prepare batter as directed. Spoon into greased, lined cupcake tins, filling ½ full.*
2. *Bake in moderate oven, 375°, about 15 to 18 minutes, or until cakes test done.*

Tangy Brown Ribs (page 105) are hearty, satisfying fare. Meaty pork spareribs in a lusty, savory sauce have an aroma that is better than a dinner bell to call the family to the table.

Fluffy Orange Rice (page 225) is a perfect accompaniment for almost any meat or poultry dish you can think of, but it is especially good with pork or ham.

Toll House Baked Beans—a zesty, hearty, main dish—only ten minutes in the Radarange Oven. (Page 185).

Salmon and Green Bean Casserole (page 69) really deserves a more glamorous name. Just read the list of luscious ingredients in the recipe.

Swiss Broccoli Custard (page 184) is an elegant way to serve a familiar vegetable and so easy to make. An equally tasty custard can be made with spinach or green beans.

For the holiday season, try acorn squash, filled with cranberries and pineapple, spiced to perfection (page 171). Lovely to look at and delicious to eat.

DANISH APPLE CAKE

¼ cup sugar
1 cup packaged biscuit mix
1 egg, beaten
¼ cup plus 1 tablespoon
  heavy cream
2 cups tart apples, peeled
  and sliced

2 tablespoons sugar
½ teaspoon cinnamon
⅛ teaspoon nutmeg
2 tablespoons melted butter
  or margarine
½ teaspoon vanilla

Stir ¼ cup sugar into biscuit mix. Blend eggs and cream; stir into dry mixture with fork. Spread soft dough on bottom of 8-inch glass cake pan that has been sprayed with vegetable oil coating. Press apples in lightly. Mix together sugar with spices, sprinkle over apples. Melt butter 15 seconds. Mix butter and vanilla. Cook in Radarange oven 6 to 7 minutes. Turn dish a quarter turn every 2 minutes. Let stand a few minutes before serving. Makes 6 to 8 servings.

Conventional Cooking:
1. *Mix batter as directed. Spread in pan. Use remaining ingredients as directed.*
2. *Bake in moderate oven, 350°, about 25 to 30 minutes.*

DATE AND NUT BREAD

¾ cup chopped pecans
1 cup chopped dates
1½ teaspoons baking soda
½ teaspoon salt
3 tablespoons shortening
¾ cup boiling water

2 medium eggs
½ teaspoon lemon extract
½ teaspoon vanilla
1 cup sugar
1½ cups sifted all-purpose
  flour

Grease or spray with vegetable oil coating 8½"x4"x 2½" glass loaf pan. Mix first four ingredients. Add shortening and water, mix lightly; let stand 20 minutes. Beat eggs lightly, beat in remaining ingredients with a fork. Add the date-nut mixture. Mix with rotary mixer until well blended, and pour into greased glass loaf pan. Cook in Radarange oven 8 minutes, turning the pan a quarter turn every 2 minutes. Let stand in pan 10 minutes; remove to cooling rack. Allow to stand overnight before slicing. Makes one loaf.

Conventional Cooking:
1. *Mix together ingredients as above.*
2. *Bake in a preheated 350° oven for 1 hour. Cool 10 minutes before removing from pan.*

FANCY CORN MUFFINS

1 cup yellow cornmeal	2 medium eggs, beaten
1 cup all-purpose flour	1 cup milk
¼ cup sugar	¼ cup vegetable oil
4 teaspoons baking powder	1 can (12 oz.) Mexicorn
¼ teaspoon chili powder	(niblets with green and
½ teaspoon salt	red peppers), drained

Mix and sift cornmeal, flour, sugar, baking powder, chili powder, and salt. Stir in eggs, milk, and oil. Beat with rotary beater until smooth, about 1 minute. Mix in corn.

Bake muffins in glass custard cups lined with baking papers. Fill papers ½ full. Bake 6 at a time, in a circle arrangement, in Radarange oven 2½ to 2¾ minutes. Remove muffins to a cooling rack. Repeat with remaining dough until all are baked. Makes 18 to 20 muffins.

Conventional Cooking:
1. *Sift and mix ingredients.*
2. *Bake in greased muffin cups in a preheated 425° oven for 15 to 20 minutes.*

FARMER'S GINGERBREAD

1 tablespoon vinegar
⅔ cup milk
2 cups sifted all-purpose
  flour
2 teaspoons baking powder
½ teaspoon baking soda
½ teaspoon salt
1½ teaspoons ginger

1 teaspoon cinnamon
½ teaspoon nutmeg
1 teaspoon allspice
⅓ cup shortening
½ cup sugar
2 eggs
1 cup molasses
1 cup whipped cream

Add vinegar to milk; let stand. Sift dry ingredients together. Cream shortening; add sugar, beat until fluffy. Beat in eggs and molasses. Add dry ingredients alternately with the milk (which will be curdled). Turn batter into 8-inch-square glass baking dish sprayed with vegetable oil coating. Cover with paper towel. Bake in Radarange oven 12 minutes, turning dish quarter turn every 2 minutes. Let stand 10 minutes before cutting in squares. Serve warm with whipped cream. Makes one 8-inch-square cake.

Conventional Cooking:
1. *Combine ingredients as directed above.*
2. *Bake in a well-greased or sprayed 8-inch-square dish in a preheated 350° oven, about 40 minutes.*

BLUEBERRY MUFFINS

2 cups all-purpose flour
⅓ cup sugar
2 teaspoons baking powder
¼ teaspoon salt
¼ teaspoon nutmeg

1 cup milk
⅓ cup vegetable oil
1 egg, beaten
1¼ cups blueberries

Sift dry ingredients together. Mix together milk, oil, and egg. Add liquid ingredients to dry ingredients; mix until all ingredients are wet (do not beat). Batter will be lumpy. Stir in blueberries. Fill lined custard cups about ½ full. Arrange 6 cups in a circle in oven, cook in Radarange oven 2½ to 3 minutes. One or two muffins may bake before the others; they can be taken out of oven. Repeat. Makes 12 muffins. Cool on rack after removing from cups.

Conventional Cooking:
1. *Prepare muffin batter as directed. Spoon into greased muffin tins, filling ¾ full.*
2. *Bake in a hot oven, 425°, 25 minutes.*

FRUITED COOKIE SQUARES

1 cup diced fruit cake mix*
(chopped glazed fruit)
1 cup chopped walnuts or
pecans
1 cup packed brown sugar
¾ cup all-purpose flour
1½ teaspoons baking
powder

¼ teaspoon salt
3 medium eggs
2 tablespoons warm water
1 teaspoon vanilla
Cinnamon sugar

Thoroughly mix first 6 ingredients. Beat eggs with water and vanilla. Stir first mixture into egg mixture; blend thoroughly. Spread mixture evenly in 8-inch-square baking dish sprayed with a vegetable oil coating. Cover with plastic wrap, cook in oven 8 to 8½ minutes. Turn pan at 2-minute intervals. Let stand 10 minutes, turn out on rack. Cut in 16 squares, dust with cinnamon-sugar. Makes 16 cookie squares.

*Or use chopped prunes, dates, or other moist dried fruits.

Conventional Cooking:
1. *Prepare batter as directed*, omitting water. *Turn into greased or sprayed pan.*
2. *Bake in a slow moderate oven, 325°, 30 minutes.*

IRISH SODA BREAD

4 cups all-purpose flour
¼ cup sugar
1 teaspoon salt
1 teaspoon baking powder
¼ cup butter or margarine

1½ cups currants
1⅓ cups buttermilk
2 medium eggs
1 teaspoon baking soda

Mix first 4 ingredients; sift into a bowl. Cut in butter with pastry blender until mixture looks like cornmeal. Stir in currants. Mix together remaining ingredients; stir into flour mixture until well moistened—do not overmix. Turn batter into a greased 2-quart round casserole or soufflé dish, cover with paper towel. Cook in Radarange oven 11 to 12 minutes, turning every 3 minutes. Let stand 10 minutes; remove to cooling rack. Makes 1 loaf.

Note: For a crisp brown top, brush with melted butter and place under broiler of conventional range for a few seconds.

Conventional Cooking:
1. Combine ingredients as directed, turn into greased casserole.
2. Bake at 375° for about 50 minutes.

MAINE ANADAMA BREAD

2 cups hot water
½ cup yellow cornmeal
1 teaspoon salt
¾ cup molasses
2 tablespoons shortening

1 package active dry yeast
½ cup warm water
  (105°–115°)
4½ to 5 cups all-purpose
  flour

Mix water, cornmeal, and salt in 2-quart casserole or bowl. Cook in Radarange oven 3 minutes, stir well; cook in oven 3 to 4 minutes more. Stir, cover, let stand 5 minutes. Stir in molasses and shortening; let cool to lukewarm. Soften yeast in warm water in a large bowl. Stir in cooled cornmeal mixture; mix well. Add flour gradually to make a stiff dough. Turn out on floured board; knead about 7 to 8 minutes until smooth. Return the dough to greased bowl, turn to grease all surfaces. Cover; let rise in warm place (85°) until doubled in bulk, about 1 hour. Divide dough in half, shape into 2 round loaves; place in 2 well-greased or sprayed 8-inch round glass cake pans or casseroles. Cover; let rise about 1 hour. Cook 1 loaf at a time in oven for 10 to 12 minutes, turning dish a quarter turn every 2 minutes. Let stand in pan 5 minutes. Turn out and cool on rack. Makes 2 8-inch loaves.

Conventional Cooking:
1. *Prepare bread as directed, reducing hot water to 1¾ cups.*
2. *After rising twice, bake in a hot oven, 400°, for 10 minutes. Reduce heat to 350°; bake 35 to 40 minutes.*

MYSTERY PUDDING CAKE

¾ cup sugar	3 tablespoons oil
1 cup sifted all-purpose flour	½ cup milk
	1 teaspoon vanilla
2 teaspoons baking powder	½ cup brown sugar, firmly packed
⅛ teaspoon salt	
1 teaspoon cinnamon	½ cup granulated sugar
½ teaspoon allspice	4 tablespoons cocoa
¼ teaspoon nutmeg	1 cup cold coffee

Mix and sift first 7 ingredients. Mix together oil, milk, and vanilla; add to dry ingredients; mix well. Pour into greased 8-inch-square baking dish. Mix together next 3 ingredients, sprinkle evenly over batter. Pour cold coffee evenly over surface. Cover with paper towel; cook in oven 8 to 9 minutes, turning dish 180° twice. Let stand 10 minutes. Serve warm with whipped cream, or coffee ice cream. Makes 8 servings.

Conventional Cooking:

1. *Mix as directed above.*
2. *Bake in a preheated 350° oven 45 minutes.*

OATMEAL MUFFINS

1½ cups quick-cooking
  rolled oats
1⅓ cups milk
1¼ cups all-purpose flour
¼ teaspoon cinnamon
¼ teaspoon nutmeg
2 teaspoons baking powder
1 teaspoon salt

2 eggs, beaten
½ cup shortening, melted
⅓ cup brown sugar, firmly
  packed
½ cup raisins
Topping:
½ teaspoon cinnamon
1 tablespoon sugar

Mix rolled oats into milk, let stand 20 to 30 minutes; stir well. Mix dry ingredients; sift into large bowl. Mix eggs and remaining ingredients (except topping), with oatmeal mixture. Make a well in the center of dry ingredients, add oatmeal all at once. Stir together just until all dry ingredients are moist. Fill lined custard cups about ½ full. Arrange 6 cups at a time in circle in Radarange oven, cook 3 to 3½ minutes. Repeat with remaining batter. Cool muffins on a rack to prevent soggy bottoms. Sprinkle tops of muffins with sugar topping. Serve warm. Makes twelve muffins.

Conventional Cooking:

1. *Prepare ingredients as indicated. Fill into greased muffin tins.*
2. *Bake in a hot oven, 400°, about 25 minutes.*

ORANGE DANISH REFRIGERATOR ROLLS

1 roll (8) refrigerated Orange Danish Rolls

Place large Browning Skillet in Radarange oven.* Preheat 2 minutes. Remove skillet from oven. Place 8 rolls on skillet, and cook, uncovered, 45 seconds. Turn rolls over with spatula, cover, and cook 2 to 2¼ minutes more. Frost while warm.

*Browning Skillet may be sprayed with vegetable oil coating before preheating.

Conventional Cooking:
1. *Separate rolls and arrange on cookie tin following package directions.*
2. *Bake as directed on package. Frost while warm.*

ORANGE GINGERBREAD

¼ cup butter or margarine	¼ teaspoon cinnamon
1 medium egg, beaten	¼ teaspoon salt
¼ cup sugar	1 tablespoon orange peel,
1¼ cups all-purpose flour	grated
¾ teaspoon baking soda	¼ cup molasses
¼ teaspoon allspice	¼ cup honey
½ teaspoon ginger	½ cup hot water

Place butter in large mixing bowl, melt in Radarange oven 30 seconds; cool. Beat in egg and sugar until well blended. Sift together dry ingredients; stir in grated peel. Mix together liquid ingredients. Add liquid alternately with dry ingredients to butter mixture. Blend well. Turn batter into sprayed 9-inch round cake dish. Cook in oven 4½ minutes, turn dish a quarter turn every 1½ minutes. Done when wooden pick inserted in center comes out clean. Let stand a few minutes before serving. Makes 8 to 10 servings.

Conventional Cooking:
1. *Mix batter as indicated. Turn into greased or sprayed 9-inch round pan.*
2. *Bake in a moderate oven, 350°, about 45 minutes.*

RUM CAKE

2 eggs
¼ teaspoon salt
1 cup sugar
1 teaspoon rum flavoring
½ teaspoon vanilla
½ cup milk

1 tablespoon butter or
margarine
1 cup sifted all-purpose
flour
1 teaspoon baking powder

In a large bowl, beat eggs until thick and light. Beat in salt, sugar, and flavoring. Mix milk and butter in 1-cup measure, heat in oven 1½ minutes. Beat into egg mixture. Mix and sift flour and baking powder; beat into egg mixture. Turn batter into well sprayed 9-inch glass cake pan or round, straight sided baking dish. Cook in Radarange oven 5 minutes, give dish a quarter turn at 1 minute intervals. Let cake stand 10 minutes; remove from pan. While still warm, spoon Coffee-Rum Syrup* carefully over surface of cake until it is all absorbed. Refrigerate cake 2 to 3 hours. Carefully split the cold cake into 2 thin layers, fill with cold Rum Cream† Filling. Spread top with thick pureed apricot preserves; decorate with whipped cream. Makes 6 to 8 servings.

*Coffee Rum Syrup:
Mix ½ cup sugar, ½ cup boiling water, and 1 tablespoon instant coffee in 1-quart bowl or casserole. Cook in Radarange oven 1 to 1½ minutes until syrup boils. Cool, add 1 tablespoon rum extract.

†Rum Cream Filling:
⅓ cup sugar
¼ cup flour
Dash salt
1 cup milk

2 egg yolks, beaten
1 teaspoon rum extract
1 teaspoon vanilla

Combine sugar, flour, and salt in bowl or small casserole. Blend in milk. Cook in Radarange oven, 2½ minutes; stir twice. Add a little of the hot sauce to egg yolks; mix well with remaining hot mixture. Cook in oven 30 seconds. Add flavorings. Chill.

Conventional Cooking:
1. *Prepare cake batter as directed. Bake in moderate oven, 350°, 35 minutes until done. Prepare syrup as directed in small saucepan. Cook over moderate heat, stirring often, about 8 to 10 minutes. Prepare filling as directed, cooking over low heat until thick, about 9 or 10 minutes. Chill.*
2. *Put cake together as directed.*

SAVORY CASSEROLE BREAD

1 cup creamy cottage cheese

1 package active dry yeast

½ cup warm water (105°–115°)

3 tablespoons sugar

2 tablespoons butter or margarine

1 teaspoon dill seed

1 tablespoon instant minced onions

½ teaspoon celery seed

1 teaspoon salt

¼ teaspoon baking soda

1 egg

2¼ to 2½ cups all-purpose flour

1 tablespoon butter, melted

½ teaspoon bottled browning sauce

Coarse salt

Heat cottage cheese in Radarange oven 45 seconds; stir well. Soften yeast in warm water in large bowl. Stir in sugar, butter, seasonings, baking soda, and warm cottage cheese; mix very well. Blend in egg. Gradually beat in flour to make a fairly stiff dough. Cover, let rise in warm place (85°) until double in bulk, about 1 hour. Punch down. Turn dough into well-greased 2½-quart round casserole; let rise about 40 minutes until double in bulk. Cook in Radarange oven 8 minutes. Turn dish a quarter turn every 2 minutes. Let stand 5 minutes in pan. Turn out on cooling rack, brush with melted butter and browning sauce. Sprinkle with coarse salt. Makes 1 loaf.

Conventional Cooking:
1. *Prepare as directed.*
2. *Bake in a moderate oven, 375°, 50 minutes.*

202

SOUTHERN CREAM CAKE

1 cup whipping cream	1 cup sugar, sifted
2 teaspoons vanilla	2 teaspoons baking powder
3 medium eggs, well beaten	½ teaspoon salt
2 cups all-purpose flour, sifted	¼ cup good sherry
	Powdered sugar

Whip cream until it holds its shape. Stir in vanilla and eggs. Mix and sift remaining ingredients (except sherry), and add a little at a time to cream mixture, folding in gently. Spoon into well sprayed china or glass 10-inch bundt cake pan. Cover with wax paper. Cook in Radarange oven 7 to 8 minutes. Turn cake a quarter turn every 2 minutes. Turn out on rack. Spoon sherry over cake, and let stand 10 to 12 minutes. Dust cake with powdered sugar. Can be served with a berry sauce, possibly strawberry. Makes 1 10-inch tube cake.

Conventional Cooking:
1. *Prepare batter as directed, spoon into greased or sprayed tube pan.*
2. *Bake in slow moderate oven, 325°, 45 to 55 minutes until the cake tests done.*

SPICED "DOUGHNUT" MUFFINS

⅓ cup vegetable oil	½ teaspoon salt
1 cup sugar, divided	½ cup milk
2 eggs	6 tablespoons butter or margarine, melted
1½ cups all-purpose flour, sifted	1 teaspoon cinnamon
1½ teaspoons baking powder	¼ teaspoon nutmeg

Mix oil with ¾ cup sugar. Beat in eggs. Mix and sift dry ingredients; add alternately with milk to creamed mixture. Spoon batter into 12 paper lined custard cups. Fill cups ½ full. Arrange 6 cups in a circle in Radarange oven; cook 2 to 2¼ minutes. Repeat for remaining 6 cups. While muffins are warm, peel off paper liners. Roll muffins in melted butter, then in remaining sugar mixed with spices. Makes 12 spiced muffins.

Conventional Cooking:
1. *Prepare batter as directed. Spoon into 12 greased muffin cups.*
2. *Bake in a moderate oven, 350°, about 20 minutes. Turn out and roll in butter and spices.*

SWISS CHOCOLATE CHERRY KUCHEN

1 cup butter or margarine	½ teaspoon baking powder
4 squares unsweetened chocolate, broken	½ teaspoon salt
2 cups sugar	1 cup canned, pitted, sour red cherries, drained
4 eggs, beaten	2 teaspoons vanilla
2 cups sifted all-purpose flour	1 cup heavy cream, whipped

Place butter and chocolate in medium bowl or glass measure; cover, cook in Radarange oven 2 to 3 minutes until chocolate is melted. Mix well. Beat sugar gradually into eggs until fluffy. Beat in chocolate mixture. Mix and sift dry ingredients, add to chocolate-egg mixture, beat well. Stir well-drained cherries and vanilla into batter. Mix well. Divide batter evenly between 2 well-sprayed 9-inch glass layer cake pans. Cover with wax paper. Cook 1 layer in oven 9 to 10 minutes, turning dish a quarter turn every 2 minutes. Let stand 10 minutes before turning out. Repeat with second layer. When cold, decorate each layer with whipped cream; cut in wedges to serve. Makes 12 to 16 servings (6 to 8 per layer).

Conventional Cooking:
1. *Prepare cake, mixing as directed above.*
2. *Bake in well-greased, floured or sprayed pans in a pre-heated, 350° oven, about 40 minutes.*

TOMATO SPICE CAKE

1¾ cups all-purpose flour
1 cup sugar
3 teaspoons baking powder
½ teaspoon each cinnamon,
  cloves, and nutmeg
½ cup soft shortening

¼ cup water
1 can (10 oz.) condensed
  tomato soup, divided
2 eggs, beaten
¾ cup raisins, chopped

Sift dry ingredients together into mixer bowl. Add shortening, water, and ½ can soup. Beat until smooth. Add remaining soup and eggs. Beat until smooth. Stir in raisins. Pour batter into a sprayed 8-inch-square dish. Cover with plastic film. Cook in Radarange oven 11 to 12 minutes, turning pan one quarter turn 3 times. Let stand 10 minutes. Cool on rack. Makes 12 servings.

Conventional Cooking:
1. Prepare cake as directed. Do not cover.
2. Bake in moderate oven, 350°, 35 to 40 minutes.

VERMONT LEMON BREAD

1¼ cups sugar, divided
2 eggs
6 tablespoons vegetable
  shortening or oil
1½ cups sifted all-purpose
  flour
1½ teaspoons baking
  powder

¼ teaspoon salt
2 teaspoons vanilla, divided
½ cup milk
1 medium lemon, grated
  peel and juice
½ teaspoon cinnamon

Beat 1 cup sugar, eggs, and shortening together until light and fluffy. Mix together and sift the dry ingredients, except cinnamon. Combine 1 teaspoon vanilla and milk. Add dry ingredients alternately with liquid to creamed mixture. Mix well. Stir in grated lemon peel. Turn batter into sprayed 8½"x4½"x2½" glass loaf pan. Cover with plastic film, cook in Radarange oven 6 minutes. Turn pan 180° after 3 minutes baking. To test doneness a wooden pick inserted in center of loaf should come out clean. Remove plastic cover. Mix lemon juice with remaining ¼ cup sugar, 1 teaspoon vanilla and cinnamon, pour over top of loaf. Let stand in pan 10 minutes; remove to cooling rack. Makes 1 loaf.

Conventional Cooking:
1. *Mix together as directed above.*
2. *Bake in 325° oven about 1 hour.*
3. *Glaze as directed and cool before serving.*

VIRGINIA SPOON BREAD

1 cup white cornmeal	*1 cup milk*
1 teaspoon salt	*3 eggs, beaten*
3 cups boiling water	*2 teaspoons baking powder*
2 tablespoons butter or margarine	

Stir cornmeal and salt into boiling water in 1½- to 2-quart casserole. Cook in Radarange oven 6 minutes, stirring several times. Beat in butter and milk, cool about 30 minutes until mixture reaches room temperature. Beat eggs until thick. Thoroughly mix eggs and baking powder into cornmeal mixture with a rotary mixer. Bake in casserole, covered with wax paper or lid, in oven for 12 minutes, turning dish a quarter turn every 3 minutes. Remove cover, let stand a few minutes before serving. Serve hot with butter. Makes 6 to 8 servings.

Conventional Cooking:
1. *Cook cornmeal and water over medium heat until thick, about 20 minutes. Beat in rest of ingredients.*
2. *Bake in a hot oven, 400°, about 50 minutes.*

WHEAT BATTER BREAD

1 package active dry yeast
1½ cups warm water
  (105°–115°)
2 tablespoons brown sugar
1 cup whole wheat flour,
  divided

2 cups all-purpose flour,
  sifted, divided
2 teaspoons salt
3 tablespoons soft short-
  ening or oil
Butter or margarine

Dissolve yeast in water in mixing bowl. Add brown sugar, ½ cup unsifted whole wheat flour, 1 cup sifted white flour, salt, and shortening. Beat 2 minutes on medium speed. Scrape down sides of bowl often. Add and mix remaining flours with mixing spoon or rubber spatula, mixing until smooth. Cover. Let rise in warm place (85°) about 45 minutes until doubled in bulk. Stir down batter; mix well for about 25 strokes. Turn into greased round 2-quart casserole. Let rise about 40 minutes. Cook in Radarange oven 8 minutes, turning dish at 2-minute intervals. Let stand in dish for 10 minutes. Cool on rack. Brush top with a little melted butter or margarine. Makes 1 round cottage loaf.

Conventional Cooking:
1. Prepare as directed.
2. Bake in a hot oven, 400°, about 45 to 50 minutes.

CHAPTER 5:

Desserts and Dessert Sauces, Too!

The Radarange microwave oven makes desserts in minutes. In fact, you can decide what to have and prepare it while the table is being cleared! Should there be a difference of opinion, the Radarange oven can prepare *two* desserts in a jiffy.

You will find a collection of dessert recipes here—some quick and easy, some that require a little more time to prepare. But the cooking is always fast—and sure—if you follow the recipe exactly.

How to defrost frozen fruits

Open original package; turn fruit into quart casserole. Cover; place in Radarange oven for the times recommended below.

Strawberries	*(10 oz. pkg.)*—1¼ to 1½ min.
Sliced Peaches	*(12 oz. pkg.)*—1½ to 1¾ min.
Raspberries	*(10 oz. pkg.)*—1½ to 1¾ min.
Pineapple Chunks	*(12 oz. pkg.)*—1½ to 2 min.
Mixed Fruit	*(10 oz. pkg.)*—1¼ to 1½ min.

Do not thaw completely . . . only until individual pieces can be separated with a fork. Serve while slightly frosty.

Cake frosting tip

When you have extra frosting for a cake, refrigerate the excess until needed. Then soften in Radarange oven to spreading consistency for approximately 5 seconds per cup.

Chocolate melting tip

You need not use a double boiler again. This is one of the many ways you can make the Radarange oven work for you. Try the following and forget your cumbersome double boiler.

Melt chocolate in its non-metallic wrapper. When a recipe calls for 1 ounce of melted chocolate, simply place the chocolate, still in its wrapper (seam side up), for 1 minute in the Radarange oven. It will soften to blending consistency. Add the chocolate directly to the cooking mixture. Measurements are more accurate as chocolate is not lost on the sides of a pan. The same method can be used to melt butter.

BAKED APPLES

4 apples (about 1½ lb.)   *Butter*
¼ cup sugar

Core apples and slice a thin circle of peel from top of each apple. Arrange apples in a 9-inch glass cake pan. Spoon 1 tablespoon sugar into each cavity, and add a small piece of butter to each apple. Cook 4 to 5 minutes in Radarange oven, or until apples are tender, depending on the type of apple. Makes 4 servings.

Variations:

Apples may be filled with mincemeat, whole cranberry sauce, or raisins and nuts. If this is done, add 1 to 2 minutes to cooking time.

Conventional Cooking:

1. *Place apples in an 8-inch baking pan with water added halfway.*
2. *Bake at 350° for 1 hour.*

CARAMEL CUSTARD

¾ cup sugar, divided　　　　*1¾ cups milk*
3 eggs, slightly beaten　　　*Nutmeg*
⅛ teaspoon salt　　　　　　*1½ cups boiling water*
1 teaspoon vanilla

Preheat small Browning Skillet in Radarange oven 2½ minutes. Add ½ cup sugar, stir well as it begins to melt. Cook in oven 1½ to 2 minutes, stirring well every 30 seconds. Quickly spoon hot caramel syrup into 6 6-ounce dessert dishes or custard cups and tilt to glaze bottom and sides of dish with syrup. Mix together remaining ¼ cup sugar with next 4 ingredients; mix well with beater. Pour into caramel-coated dishes. Sprinkle with nutmeg. Set cups in 2-quart oblong glass casserole, pour boiling water around base of cups. Cook uncovered in oven 6 minutes, turn dish around 180° after 3 minutes cooking time. One or more custards may become firm before others, and can be removed as soon as done. Cook remaining custards 30 seconds to 1 minute longer. Delicious warm or cold. Makes 6 servings.

Conventional Cooking:

1. *Caramelize ½ cup sugar in small heavy pan over very low heat. Stir constantly with a long-handled spoon for about 4 to 6 minutes until the sugar is melted and straw*

color. Coat custard dishes as directed above, fill with custard sauce, add dash nutmeg.
2. Bake in a pan with boiling water around cups at 325° for about 30 minutes.

CARAMEL PUMPKIN FLAN

1¼ cups sugar, divided
1 cup canned pumpkin
1 teaspoon cinnamon
¼ teaspoon ginger
¼ teaspoon nutmeg

½ teaspoon vanilla
½ teaspoon rum extract
5 eggs, beaten
2 cups light cream

Preheat Browning Skillet in Radarange oven 4½ minutes. Add 1 cup sugar, stir well. Cook in oven 2½ to 3 minutes, stirring at 1-minute intervals until sugar is melted, smooth, and a nice caramel color. Immediately turn the caramel into a 9-inch glass cake pan. Turn the dish round and round (use pot holders) until inside is coated with caramel (liquid sugar). Let the caramel set. Mix together pumpkin with remaining sugar, spices, and flavorings. Add eggs to cream, stir into pumpkin mixture. Pour pumpkin mixture into prepared dish. Set in larger dish of hot water. Cook in oven 12 minutes, turn dish a quarter turn every 3 minutes. Custard should be set; knife inserted near edge comes out clean. Remove from hot water to cooling rack. Let stand until cool, then chill. To serve, run a spatula around the sides of dish, carefully turn out in deep serving plate. Serve with whipped cream. Makes 8 servings.

Conventional Cooking:
1. Caramelize 1 cup sugar in heavy fry pan over very low heat. Stir constantly for 8 to 10 minutes, until sugar is melted and straw colored. Coat 9-inch glass cake pan as directed above.
2. Prepare custard, pour into caramelized cake pan. Set in larger pan with hot water.
3. Bake at 325° for 60 to 65 minutes.

CHOCOLATE BAKED CUSTARD

½ cup semi-sweet chocolate
   pieces
1⅔ cups undiluted evapo-
   rated milk
1 cup water, cool

4 medium eggs
½ cup sugar
½ teaspoon salt
½ teaspoon vanilla
1 cup boiling water

Mix together chocolate pieces, evaporated milk, and water in 1-quart glass measure or bowl. Cook in Radarange oven 4 to 5 minutes, or until chocolate is melted. Beat eggs, sugar, salt, and vanilla together with rotary beater until well blended. Pour in chocolate mixture, stirring constantly. Beat until well mixed. Pour into 8 custard cups. Set 4 cups in 8-inch-square glass cake dish, add 1 cup boiling water to cake dish. Bake in oven 2 minutes, turn dish 180°, cook 1 minute more. Repeat with next 4 custards. Cool cups on wire rack. Makes 8 servings.

Conventional Cooking:
1. *Mix as directed above; pour into custard cups. Set cups in baking dish, add 2 cups boiling water around base of cups.*
2. *Bake at 350°, about 30 minutes.*

FRUIT SURPRISE PUDDING

⅓ cup butter or margarine
1 cup sugar
2½ cups all-purpose flour
2 teaspoons baking powder
½ teaspoon salt
1 cup milk
1 teaspoon vanilla
½ cup maraschino cherries,
   drained and chopped

1 can (8 oz.) crushed pineapple, drained
1 tablespoon butter or
   margarine
2 cups light brown sugar,
   firmly packed
½ cup boiling water

In large mixing bowl cream butter; beat in sugar gradually until light and fluffy. Mix and sift dry ingredients; mix milk and vanilla. Add dry ingredients alternately with milk to sugar mixture. Spread batter in 2-quart baking pan sprayed with vegetable coating, sprinkle with cherries and pineapple, dot with butter. Spread brown sugar in even layer over fruit, pour boiling water over all. Cover with wax paper. Cook in Radarange oven 10 to 12 minutes. Turn pan halfway around 4 times. Let stand, covered, 10 minutes. Serve warm with whipped cream. Makes 8 servings.

Conventional Cooking:
1. *Prepare pudding as directed.*
2. *Bake in a moderate oven, 350°, about 1 hour or until cake tests done.*

INSTANT FROSTING FANCIES

2 tablespoons butter or
 margarine
¼ cup milk*

1 package creamy frosting
 mix

Heat butter and milk in small glass casserole in Radarange oven until mixture begins to simmer, about 1 minute. Stir in dry frosting mix. Heat 1 minute, stirring every 15 seconds. For fudge, add ½ cup chopped nuts to chocolate mix; pour into greased 8-inch-square glass pan. Refrigerate 1 hour. For wafers, drop by teaspoonsful onto waxed paper. For clusters stir in 1½ cups salted peanuts, drop by teaspoonsful on waxed paper. Makes 36 pieces.

*If using golden caramel frosting mix, reduce milk to 3 tablespoons.

Conventional Cooking:
1. *Mix as directed in small saucepan.*
2. *Stir over moderate heat for 3 to 4 minutes. Proceed as directed for desired candy.*

MOCHA BREAD CUSTARD

½ cup semi-sweet chocolate
   pieces
1 cup strong coffee (1 tablespoon instant and 1 cup
   boiling water)
1 cup milk
1 tablespoon melted butter
   or margarine

3 eggs, beaten
¼ cup sugar
¼ teaspoon salt
½ teaspoon vanilla
1½ cups white bread cubes
¼ teaspoon cinnamon
1 cup boiling water

Place chocolate pieces in medium-size bowl, cover; cook in Radarange oven 2 minutes until chocolate softens. Add coffee, milk, and butter; cook in oven 3 minutes. Mix eggs, sugar, salt, and vanilla. Stir hot chocolate mixture into egg mixture. Place bread cubes in 1½-quart casserole; pour chocolate egg mixture on cubes, sprinkle with cinnamon. Set casserole in larger pan, add 1 cup boiling water to pan. Cook in oven 9 to 10 minutes, turning 180° 3 times. Let stand 10 minutes. Serve warm or cold with whipped cream. Makes 5 to 6 servings.

Conventional Cooking:
1. *Scald milk over medium heat, stir in chocolate and coffee. Heat until chocolate melts. Prepare remainder of recipe as directed.*
2. *Bake in moderate oven, 325°, about 50 minutes, or until set and firm to touch.*

NORWEGIAN PRUNE DESSERT

½ pound large tender
   pitted prunes
1½ cups boiling water
½ cup sugar
½ cup walnuts, chopped

1 tablespoon lemon juice
½ teaspoon cinnamon
2 tablespoons cornstarch
¼ cup sherry or port

Boil water in 1½-quart covered casserole 4 minutes in Radarange oven. Add prunes. Let stand covered 2 hours. Remove prunes from liquid. To liquid add sugar, walnuts,

214

lemon juice, cinnamon, and cornstarch. Cook, uncovered, 1½ minutes, stir well. Cook 1 minute more till thickened. Add wine and prunes. Chill. Spoon into sherbet glasses; serve topped with almond-flavored whipped cream. Makes 6 servings.

Conventional Cooking:
1. *Add prunes to boiling water. Let stand covered 2 hours. Remove prunes from liquid, add remaining ingredients to liquid.*
2. *Heat on medium heat till thickened. Stir often. Add prunes and wine and chill to serve.*

SPICED FRUIT COMPOTE

2 medium-size apples, cored and peeled
1 can (1 lb.) pear halves* —reserve 2 tablespoons pear syrup

½ cup whole berry cranberry sauce
⅛ teaspoon cinnamon
Pinch cloves
Pinch allspice

Cut apples in eighths; pear halves in lengthwise halves. Layer apples and pears in 1½-quart casserole. Mix together cranberry sauce, spices, and 2 tablespoons pear syrup. Spoon over fruit. Cook covered in Radarange oven 8 to 10 minutes until apples are tender. Serve warm or cold. Makes 6 servings.

*If desired, substitute same size can pineapple chunks or apricot halves.

Conventional Cooking:
1. *Combine fruits and juice in a 1½-quart saucepan.*
2. *Cook over medium heat 30 to 35 minutes.*

ST. CROIX BAKED BANANAS

6 medium green-tipped bananas
3 tablespoons lime juice
⅓ cup honey
⅓ cup sherry or rum

3 tablespoons butter or margarine
¼ cup red currant jelly
½ cup flaked coconut

Peel bananas, place in shallow baking dish; brush all over with lime juice. Mix honey and wine, spoon over bananas; dot with butter. Cook in oven 8 minutes. Turn dish completely around after 4 minutes and spoon syrup over bananas. Dot with jelly, sprinkle with coconut. Serve warm. Makes 6 servings.

Conventional Cooking:
1. Prepare as directed.
2. Bake in a greased shallow baking dish 30 minutes at 400°.

Dessert Sauces

APPLE PECAN SYRUP

3 tablespoons butter or margarine	½ teaspoon cinnamon
1 cup maple syrup	2 cups apples, peeled and very thinly sliced
Dash salt	¼ cup pecans, chopped

Mix together butter, syrup, salt, and cinnamon in bowl or 1½-quart casserole. Cook in Radarange oven 2 minutes. Add apples, cover; cook in oven 3 to 4 minutes, stirring twice. Stir in nuts. Serve warm with waffles, pancakes, or french toast. Makes 6 servings.

Conventional Cooking:
1. Mix first 4 ingredients in saucepan. Bring to boil over moderate heat. Add apple.
2. Cook covered over low heat for about 10 minutes. Remove cover, continue to cook 5 minutes, or more. Stir in nuts and serve hot.

APPLE TOPPING SAUCE

6 medium tart apples	1 tablespoon orange peel, fresh grated
½ cup granulated sugar	
½ cup brown sugar, firmly packed	3 tablespoons butter or margarine
½ teaspoon nutmeg	½ cup hot water or apple juice
1 tablespoon lemon peel, fresh grated	

216

Pare and core apples, cut into very thin slices. Place in 2-quart casserole. Mix together sugars, nutmeg, and peel; sprinkle over apples. Dot with butter, pour hot liquid over all. Cover; cook in Radarange oven 8 to 10 minutes, stirring at 3 minute intervals. Let stand, covered, 10 minutes. Serve warm over vanilla ice cream. Makes about 2 cups.

Conventional Cooking:
1. *Combine ingredients in heavy saucepan. Cook over medium heat about 5 minutes. Mix well.*
2. *Simmer, covered, about 30 minutes, stirring frequently to prevent burning.*

CUSTARD SAUCE

4 egg yolks
⅓ cup sugar
Dash salt

1½ cups milk
½ cup evaporated milk
1 teaspoon vanilla

Beat egg yolks in 1½-quart bowl or casserole. Mix in sugar and salt until well blended. Stir in milk and evaporated milk. Cook in Radarange oven about 2½ minutes, stirring at 30 second intervals. Add flavoring. Chill before serving. Makes about 2¼ cups.

Rum Custard Sauce:
Follow above recipe. Reduce vanilla to ½ teaspoon, stir in 1 teaspoon rum flavoring.

Sherry Custard Sauce:
Follow recipe above. Reduce vanilla to ½ teaspoon, stir in 1 teaspoon sherry flavoring.

Lemon Custard Sauce:
Follow above recipe. Stir in 1 teaspoon lemon extract, ½ teaspoon grated lemon peel.

Conventional Cooking:
1. *Mix as directed in top part of double boiler.*
2. *Cook over simmering water. Stir until thick and smooth, about 12 to 15 minutes.*

FRUIT SAUCE

1 package (10 oz.) frozen
   sliced strawberries,
   thawed
¼ cup sugar

1 tablespoon cornstarch*
½ cup white, rosé, or fruit-
   flavored wine

Place berries in 1-quart casserole. Mix sugar and cornstarch, stir into berries. Cook in Radarange oven 2 minutes, stirring twice. Stir in wine, cook in oven 1 minute, stirring twice. Chill before serving. Makes about 2 cups.

*This is a thin sauce. For a thicker sauce use 2 tablespoons cornstarch.

Conventional Cooking:
1. Add berries to mixed sugar and cornstarch, cook till thickened.
2. Stir in wine, cook on low heat about 5 minutes more.

PINK RHUBARB SAUCE

2 cups rhubarb (cut into 1-
   inch pieces)
2 to 3 tablespoons water
Dash salt

½ cup sugar
1 piece stick cinnamon
Red food color

Place rhubarb, water, and salt in 2-quart casserole. Cover; cook in oven 4 minutes, gently stirring twice. Add sugar and cinnamon; cook in oven 1 minute. Add few drops food coloring. Let stand, covered, until cool. Remove cinnamon stick. Chill before serving. Makes 4 servings.

Conventional Cooking:
1. Combine ½ cup water and sugar in a saucepan, bring to a boil. Cook 2 to 3 minutes. Add salt, cinnamon, and rhubarb. Reduce heat.
2. Cook over low heat about 5 minutes until rhubarb is tender.

VANILLA SAUCE

3 tablespoons butter or
   margarine
½ cup sugar
2 egg yolks, beaten

½ cup boiling water
1 teaspoon vanilla (or more
   to taste)

Heat butter in bowl or 1-quart casserole in Radarange oven 30 seconds. Add sugar; beat with wire whisk until light. Beat in egg yolks and boiling water. Cook in oven 2 minutes, stirring at 30-second intervals. Stir in vanilla. Serve hot. Makes 1 scant cup.

Lemon Sauce: Prepare as above, omit vanilla. Stir in ½ teaspoon lemon extract, 1 tablespoon lemon juice.

Conventional Cooking:
1. *In the top of a double boiler, soften butter, beat in sugar until fluffy. Beat in egg yolks. Slowly beat in hot water.*
2. *Cook over simmering water, stirring continuously, until thickened. Stir in vanilla.*

CHAPTER 6:

A Miscellany of Good Things to Eat

Cereals, Pasta, Sandwiches, Sauces, Dressings,
Candy, and Beverages

The Radarange oven is both versatile and labor saving in a variety of ways. Many foods that used to require stirring constantly for long periods can now be made in a matter of minutes. You just reach into the cool oven when a stir or two is necessary.

Here's a variety of good things that you can cook with ease.

HOW TO COOK PASTA

2 cups pasta (macaroni,   3 teaspoons salt
  noodles, or spaghetti)   4 cups boiling water

Place pasta and salt in 2½-quart casserole. For lasagna and other wide flat pastas use a 9"x5"x3" loaf pan. Stir in boiling water. Cook in Radarange oven 6 minutes. Stir well, cover, let stand 10 minutes. Drain. Makes 5 to 6 cups cooked.

Conventional Cooking:
1. *To 3 quarts boiling water add 1 tablespoon salt.*
2. *Gradually add 8 ounces (about 2 cups) macaroni or spaghetti or 8 ounces (about 4 cups) of noodles. Cook uncovered in rapidly boiling water until tender.*

HOW TO COOK RICE

2½ cups water   1 teaspoon salt
1 cup long grain rice

In a 2-quart glass casserole, bring water to boil. Stir in salt and rice. Cover and cook in Radarange oven for 7 minutes. Let stand covered for 10 minutes longer. Fluff rice with a fork before serving. Makes 6 servings.

Conventional Cooking:
1. *Bring 2½ cups of water to boil, stir in 1 cup rice, 1 teaspoon salt.*
2. *Cover tightly and simmer 20 minutes. Remove from heat, let stand covered until all water is absorbed, about 5 minutes.*

BULGARIAN PILAF

1 cup onion (1 medium onion), chopped
1 cup celery, chopped
1 teaspoon rosemary, crushed
½ teaspoon curry powder
¼ cup vegetable oil
4 envelopes instant chicken broth or 4 chicken bouillon cubes
4 cups boiling water

1 cup cracked wheat (Bulgar)
¼ cup seedless raisins
¼ cup dried apricots, peaches, or apples, chopped
3 tablespoons butter or margarine
¾ cup long grain rice, cooked (p. 221)
1 tablespoon sugar

Place vegetables, seasonings, and oil in 2-quart casserole, cook, uncovered, in oven 7 minutes. Add raisins, dried fruit, and water; cook in oven 2 minutes. Stir in cracked wheat; cook, uncovered, in oven 7 minutes. Add raisins, dried fruit, and butter; mix to distribute fruit. Cover; cook in oven 5 minutes. Stir in cooked rice and sugar. Let stand, covered, 10 to 15 minutes. Fluff mixture with fork before serving. Very good with barbecued chicken. Makes 6 to 8 servings.

Conventional Cooking:
1. Sauté vegetables, seasonings, and oil in heavy fry pan over medium heat till vegetables are soft.
2. In 2- to 2½-quart saucepan, boil water, add chicken bouillon. Stir in cracked wheat, vegetables, fruit, and rice. Cook over medium heat, 1 hour.
3. Remove from heat, add butter and sugar. Let stand 10 to 15 minutes before serving.

BUTTERED BREAD CRUMBS

1 slice of bread   Butter or margarine

Butter slice of bread on both sides. Break into crumb-size pieces. Preheat small Browning Skillet in Radarange oven 1 minute. Remove skillet from oven. Place crumbs in skillet. Cook, uncovered, in oven 1 minute, stirring once.

Conventional Cooking:
1. Prepare as directed.
2. Brown buttered bread crumbs in a small pan. Stir to prevent burning.

CHEESE AND ASPARAGUS SANDWICH

2 slices white bread   1 tablespoon mayonnaise
2 slices American cheese   Salt and pepper to taste
10 to 12 cooked or canned   Dash dry mustard
   asparagus spears   Paprika
1 egg, separated

Toast bread lightly. Place toast in small glass utility dish. Top each piece with slice of cheese. Arrange asparagus spears on cheese. Beat egg white until stiff. Beat yolk; add mayonnaise, salt, pepper, and mustard; fold in beaten egg white. Spoon mixture over asparagus, sprinkle with paprika. Cook 2 minutes in Radarange oven. Turn dish completely around after 1 minute. Makes 2 servings.

Conventional Cooking:
1. Prepare as directed.
2. Bake in a moderate oven, 375°, about 9 to 10 minutes.

CORNED BEEF HASH SANDWICHES

2 tablespoons butter or
  margarine
4 slices rye or white bread
1 cup canned corned beef
  hash

½ cup sharp cheddar
  cheese, shredded
4 tablespoons catchup

Butter bread on 1 side. Spread unbuttered side of each slice with ¼ cup hash; top with cheese and catchup. Heat large Browning Skillet in Radarange oven 2½ minutes. Place two pieces of open-face sandwiches in skillet, butter side down. Cover, cook in oven 1½ minutes until cheese melts and hash is heated through. To cook other two pieces of sandwich, pre-heat Browning Skillet 1¼ minutes. Cook sandwiches 1½ minutes. Makes 2 servings.

Conventional Cooking:
1. Prepare open face sandwiches as directed. Heat heavy skillet, add sandwiches butter side down.
2. Cook about 4 to 5 minutes uncovered. Then cover; cook about 2 minutes until cheese melts.

EASY LASAGNA

¾ pound lasagna noodles
  (12 oz.)
2 teaspoons salt
6 cups boiling water
Lasagna sauce (page 232)

1 pound ricotta cheese
⅓ pound mozzarella
  cheese, diced
½ cup Parmesan cheese,
  grated

Spread noodles in 2-quart oblong dish. Add 2 teaspoons salt to 6 cups boiling water. Pour over noodles. Separate noodles with a fork (they must all be completely moistened). Cover, cook in Radarange oven 10 minutes. Again carefully separate with a fork. Cover, let stand 10 minutes; drain. Using same oblong dish, spread overlapping layer of noodles on bottom. Top with layer of lasagna sauce. Dot with ricotta and mozzarella cheese. Sprinkle with Parmesan cheese. Repeat until all ingredients are used, ending with cheese. Cover, cook in oven 10 minutes, turning dish around completely after 5 minutes. Let stand, covered, 5 to 10 minutes before serving. Makes 6 servings.

Conventional Cooking:
1. *Cook noodles in 6 cups boiling salted water, uncovered, till tender, about 10 to 12 minutes. Layer lasagna as directed above.*
2. *Bake at 350° for about 45 minutes.*

FLUFFY ORANGE RICE

1 cup celery, chopped
¼ cup scallions,
   thinly sliced
¼ cup butter or margarine
2 tablespoons orange juice
   concentrate

1¼ cups hot water
½ teaspoon salt
Dash cinnamon
1⅓ cups packaged pre-
   cooked rice

Mix celery, scallions, and butter in 2-quart casserole; cook in Radarange oven 5 minutes, stirring twice. Add next 4 ingredients, mix well; cook in oven 5 minutes. Stir in pre-cooked rice; cover, let stand 5 minutes. Makes 4 servings.

Conventional Cooking:
1 *Sauté first three ingredients in small heavy fry pan until onions are limp and tender.*
2. *Boil water in 2-quart saucepan. Add sautéed ingredients, orange juice, and seasoning. Stir. Add pre-cooked rice. Cover and let stand for 5 minutes.*

GREEN RICE

2½ cups boiling water
1 cup long grain rice
1 teaspoon salt
½ cup parsley, minced
½ cup scallions, minced
¼ cup green pepper,
   minced

2 tablespoons butter or
   margarine
Salt and pepper to
   taste
½ cup dairy sour cream

Mix water, rice, and salt in 2-quart casserole. Cover; cook in Radarange oven 7 minutes. Let stand, covered, 10 minutes. Sauté next 3 ingredients in butter in medium glass bowl in oven, 3 minutes; then mix with remaining ingredients into rice. Cover; cook in oven 1 to 2 minutes. Fluff with fork before serving. Makes 6 servings.

Conventional Cooking:
1. *Bring water to a boil, stir in rice and salt. Cover.*
2. *Cook over medium heat, covered, for about 25 minutes, fluff and let stand few minutes to make sure all water is absorbed. Stir in remaining ingredients. Cover and let stand few minutes. Fluff with fork before serving.*

HOT MEXICAN RICE

½ cup raw long grain rice	2 teaspoons salt
1 green pepper, diced	¼ teaspoon seasoned
1 cup chopped onion	pepper
1 garlic clove, minced	1 tablespoon chili powder
1 small hot chili pepper, chopped	1 can (1 lb.) stewed tomatoes
¼ cup vegetable oil	¾ cup seedless raisins
1 pound ground beef	¼ cup pine nuts

Heat Browning Skillet in Radarange oven 4½ minutes. Mix first 5 ingredients with oil in skillet; cook in oven 3 minutes, stirring several times. Add meat, cook in oven 3 minutes. Stir in remaining ingredients; cover, cook in oven 9 to 10 minutes. Let stand, covered, 10 minutes. Fluff with fork before serving. Makes 4 servings.

Conventional Cooking:
1. *Sauté first 5 ingredients in oil in a hot skillet. Add beef; cook until all the red disappears. Add remaining ingredients.*
2. *Cook over medium heat, covered, for about 25 minutes, stirring frequently. If necessary add a little hot water as needed.*

QUICK GRITS

1 cup quick grits   4 cups boiling water
1 teaspoon salt

Measure grits and salt into 2-quart baking pan. Pour boiling water over grits. Cook, uncovered, in Radarange oven 5 minutes, stirring after 2½ minutes. Cover; let stand 5 minutes. Top each serving with a pat of butter or margarine. Makes 6 servings.

Conventional Cooking:
1. Prepare as directed, using 3½ cups water.
2. Cook over medium heat, stirring frequently, until thick, about 15 minutes.

ROMAN NOODLES

1 onion, chopped   ½ teaspoon salt
1 green pepper, chopped   ⅛ teaspoon pepper
¼ cup butter or margarine   8 ounces noodles, cooked
1 can (4 oz.) sliced mush-   (see page 221)
  rooms, drained   1 cup canned peas, drained
1 can (15 oz.) tomato sauce   Grated Parmesan cheese
¼ teaspoon powdered
  thyme

Cook onion, green pepper, and butter in medium bowl in Radarange oven 3 minutes; stir once after 1½ minutes. Combine with mushrooms, tomato sauce, and seasonings in 2½-quart casserole. Cook in oven 2 minutes. Add drained cooked noodles, cover, cook 5 minutes more. Stir in peas, cover, let stand 5 minutes. Sprinkle with Parmesan cheese. Makes 4 to 6 servings.

Conventional Cooking:
1. *Sauté onion and pepper in butter. Combine with mushrooms, tomato sauce, and seasonings in casserole. Stir in cooked noodles.*
2. *Bake in a moderate oven, 350°, about 35 to 40 minutes. Stir in peas and sprinkle with cheese during last 5 minutes baking time.*

TOASTED PEANUT APPLE SANDWICHES

1 jar (6 oz.) peanut butter	*8 slices frozen French toast*
½ cup canned applesauce	*Soft butter or margarine*

Blend peanut butter and applesauce; spread mixture on 4 slices toast. Top with remaining slices to make 4 sandwiches. Butter sandwiches lightly on both sides. Heat Browning Skillet in Radarange oven 4½ minutes. Place 2 sandwiches in skillet. Cook in oven 2 minutes. Turn sandwiches over; cook in oven 3 minutes. Repeat with remaining 2 sandwiches. Makes 4 sandwiches. Eat with knife and fork; add syrup if desired.

Conventional Cooking:
1. *Prepare sandwiches as indicated.*
2. *Cook on skillet or griddle to brown both sides, about 8 to 9 minutes.*

TURKEY "LEFTOVER" BUNS

6 hamburger buns, toasted	*¼ cup salted peanuts, chopped*
1 cup cooked turkey*, chopped	*1 hard-cooked egg*
1 tablespoon instant minced onion	*½ cup mayonnaise*
1 teaspoon instant minced parsley	*Salt and pepper*
	⅓ cup sharp cheese, shredded

Place bottom half of buns on paper towel-lined tray or plate big enough to hold 6 filled buns. Mix together remaining ingredients; spread on buns. Cook in Radarange oven 3 minutes. Add tops to make 6 "bunwiches." Makes 6 servings.

*Or any leftover cooked poultry or meat.

Conventional Cooking:
1. *Toast buns. Combine remaining ingredients to make filling. Heat filling, spoon onto buns, and add top to make "bunwiches."*
2. *Or, combine filling and buns to make 6 "bunwiches." Place on cookie tin, bake in a hot oven, 400°, 8 to 10 minutes.*

WILD RICE STUFFING

½ cup sliced almonds
2 tablespoons butter or margarine
1 can or jar (11 oz.) mandarin orange segments

Water
1 package (6 oz.) white and wild rice mix

Mix almonds and butter in 1½-quart casserole. Cook in Radarange oven 4 minutes, stirring twice. Drain juice from orange segments into 2-cup measure. Add enough water to make 2 cups liquid. Add to casserole. Stir in rice mixture with seasoning packet. Cover; cook in oven 13 minutes, stirring mixture once. Lightly stir in drained orange segments. Let stand, covered, 10 minutes before serving. Makes 4 servings.

Conventional Cooking:
1. *Sauté almonds in hot butter. Combine in casserole with liquid, rice, and seasonings.*
2. *Cover. Bake in moderate oven, 350°, 45 to 50 minutes. Stir in orange segments.*

CRANBERRY SAUCE

1 pound cranberries   1 cup water
2 cups sugar

Rinse and drain cranberries, remove soft berries and stems. Place water and sugar in 3-quart covered casserole and stir well. Add cranberries. Cook in Radarange oven 8 minutes, or until the berries have popped and the mixture has boiled up to almost the top of the dish. Allow berries to cook undisturbed. Makes 1 quart.

Conventional Cooking:
1. Combine sugar and water in saucepan. Cook over high heat 5 minutes.
2. Add cranberries, cook over medium heat until all berries pop, about 5 to 6 minutes.

HOLLANDAISE SAUCE

¼ cup butter or margarine   ½ teaspoon dry mustard
¼ cup light cream   ¼ teaspoon salt
2 egg yolks, slightly beaten   Dash Tabasco sauce
1 tablespoon lemon juice

Melt butter in 4-cup glass measure in Radarange oven 1 minute. Stir in remaining ingredients. Cook in oven 1 minute, stirring every 15 seconds. Stir briskly with wire whisk, until light and fluffy. Serve hot or cold. Makes about ⅔ cup, or enough for 4 servings on vegetables.

Conventional Cooking:
1. In top section of double boiler, melt butter over low heat. Add cream and egg yolks.
2. Cook over simmering water, stirring continously until thickened. Stir in lemon juice and seasonings.

LEMON SAUCE
(for fish)

2 tablespoons butter or margarine
2 tablespoons flour
½ teaspoon salt
1 egg yolk
½ cup light cream

1 cup fish broth
¼ cup lemon juice
2 tablespoons parsley, chopped
Dash Tabasco sauce

Melt butter in a 1-quart bowl in Radarange oven 30 seconds. Blend in flour and salt. Beat egg yolk into cream, and add gradually to flour mixture, stirring constantly. Cook in oven 45 seconds. Stir very well. Blend in remaining ingredients. Cook in oven 1½ minutes. Stir well, and cook 30 seconds more. Makes 6 to 8 servings (about 1½ cups).

Conventional Cooking:
1. *Prepare as for White Sauce, stirring continuously.*
2. *Blend in lemon juice and egg yolks last, cook and stir over low heat until thickened.*

NEW BARBECUE SAUCE

2 tablespoons butter or margarine
4 tablespoons onion, chopped
1 garlic clove, crushed
1 teaspoon Worcestershire sauce
1 cup catchup

⅛ teaspoon pepper
½ cup strong coffee
2 tablespoons vinegar
2 tablespoons sugar
2 tablespoons lemon juice
1 teaspoon dry mustard
½ teaspoon salt
½ cup celery, chopped

Melt butter in 1½-quart casserole 30 seconds in Radarange oven. Cook the onions in the butter 1½ minutes till tender.

Add the remaining ingredients. Cook, covered, 3 minutes; stir well. Cook covered 3 minutes more so flavors can blend. Makes 2 cups.

Conventional Cooking:
1. *Sauté onions in butter till tender. Add remaining ingredients.*
2. *Cook uncovered over medium low heat 15 to 20 minutes. Stir often.*

QUICK LASAGNE SAUCE

1 pound sweet or hot Italian sausage	*1 can (15½ oz.) marinara or tomato spaghetti sauce*
½ pound lean ground beef	*1 8-ounce can tomato sauce*
½ cup onion, chopped	*½ teaspoon oregano*
¼ cup green pepper, chopped	*¼ teaspoon basil*
1 garlic clove, minced	*¼ teaspoon fennel seed*
	Salt and pepper to taste

Heat Browning Skillet in Radarange oven 4½ minutes. Remove sausage meat from casing, break into small pieces. Add sausage and ground beef to skillet, cook in oven 4 minutes; stir once. Drain fat. Add onions, green pepper, and garlic; mix well. Cook in oven 2 minutes. Stir in remaining ingredients. Cook in oven 3 minutes, stirring several times. Makes about 3 cups sauce.

Conventional Cooking:
1. *Cut or break up sausage, and brown the sausage and the ground beef a few minutes in 1 tablespoon hot oil. Add onion, green pepper, and garlic. Simmer 4 to 5 minutes. Pour off excess fat, stir in sauce and seasonings.*
2. *Cover, cook over medium heat about 10 to 15 minutes.*

SHRIMP SAUCE
(for fish)

1 cup medium White Sauce
(page 235)
½ cup dairy sour cream
1 tablespoon prepared
mustard
1 teaspoon curry powder

½ teaspoon sugar
1 cup cooked shrimp,
finely diced
1 tablespoon capers,
chopped

Mix all ingredients thoroughly in small glass bowl; chill to serve cold. To serve hot,* cover, cook in Radarange oven 1½ minutes, stirring at 30 second intervals. Makes about 2 cups.

*Sauce should be at room temperature before cooking.

Conventional Cooking:
1. Mix as directed and chill to serve cold.
2. To serve hot, mix as directed, and simmer over low heat to heat through. Stir frequently.

SOUR CREAM DRESSING

½ cup sugar
3 tablespoons flour
1 teaspoon dry mustard
1 egg, slightly beaten
1 cup milk

½ cup vinegar
1 tablespoon butter or
margarine
1 teaspoon salt
1 cup dairy sour cream

Combine first 5 ingredients; cook in Radarange oven 3 minutes, or until mixture thickens. Stir after 2½ minutes. Stir in vinegar and butter. Cook 1 minute, stir once. Cool. When mixture is cold stir in salt and fold in sour cream. Serve over vegetable salad or lettuce wedges. Makes 2⅔ cups.

Conventional Cooking:
1. Mix first 5 ingredients in saucepan.
2. Stir over moderate heat until blended and thickened, about 10 minutes. Slowly stir in vinegar, add butter. Continue to stir over low heat until thick. Cool mixture. Season to taste with salt. Fold in sour cream.

TOMATO SAUCE
(for fish)

2 tablespoons butter or margarine	1 tablespoon flour
2 tablespoons finely minced celery	1 teaspoon salt
	1 cup tomato juice
2 tablespoons finely minced onion	1 tablespoon brown sugar
	Pinch allspice

Melt butter in a 1-quart bowl or casserole in Radarange oven 30 seconds. Stir in celery and onion. Cook in oven 1½ minutes. Blend in flour and salt. Add tomato juice, sugar, and allspice, stirring constantly. Cook in oven 2 minutes, stirring after 1 minute. Serve hot over fish.* Makes 4 servings (about 1 cup).

*Sauce may be strained if desired.

Conventional Cooking:
1. *Simmer celery and onion in hot butter few minutes. Proceed as for white sauce, then add rest of ingredients.*
2. *Cook and stir over medium heat until thickened. Strain if desired.*

VERY QUICK LEMON-BUTTER SAUCE

½ cup butter or margarine (1 stick)	½ teaspoon salt
Juice of 1 lemon	Dash Tabasco sauce

In small bowl, cook butter in Radarange oven 45 seconds, or until melted; stir in remaining ingredients. Serve hot. Makes ¾ cup.

Conventional Cooking:
1. *Combine ingredients in saucepan.*
2. *Cook until butter melts and bubbles. Mix well, serve hot.*

WHITE SAUCE

#1—Thin

1 tablespoon butter or margarine
1 tablespoon flour
½ teaspoon salt
1 cup milk

#2—Medium

2 tablespoons butter or margarine
2 tablespoons flour
½ teaspoon salt
1 cup milk

#3—Thick

4 tablespoons butter or margarine
4 tablespoons flour
½ teaspoon salt
1 cup milk

Basic Instructions

Melt butter in bowl or 1-quart casserole in Radarange oven 30 seconds. Stir in flour and salt to make a smooth paste. Add milk gradually, stirring constantly. Cook, uncovered, in oven 1 minute. Stir well. Cook 1½ to 2 minutes longer, stirring at the end of every 30 seconds. Makes about 1 cup.

Conventional Cooking:
1. *Melt butter in saucepan over low heat. Stir in flour and salt. Cook and stir to make a smooth paste. Add milk gradually, stirring constantly.*
2. *Continue to cook and stir about 4 to 5 minutes.*

CREAMY NUT FUDGE

2 packages (6 oz. each)
semi-sweet chocolate
pieces
1 can (14 oz.) sweetened
condensed milk

Dash salt
1 teaspoon vanilla
½ cup walnuts,
chopped

Place chocolate in 2-quart bowl or glass measure, cook in Radarange oven 1½ minutes; stir. Add condensed milk and salt. Cook in oven 1 minute. Stir in vanilla and nuts. Immediately turn mixture into buttered 8-inch-square pan, chill until firm; about 2 hours. Makes about 1 pound.

Coconut Crunch Fudge:
Substitute ½ cup flaked coconut and ½ cup crisp rice cereal for 1 cup nutmeats in recipe.

Conventional Cooking:
1. *Melt chocolate pieces on the top of a double boiler over simmering water. Add condensed milk and salt. Stir until blended; cook a few minutes more.*
2. *Remove from heat; add vanilla and chopped nuts. Chill until firm in a buttered 8-inch-square pan.*

GRAPE JELLY

6 cups Concord grapes
2 cups apples, diced
1 cup water

¾ cup sugar for each cup
juice

Combine grapes, apples, and water in 4-quart glass dish; cover. Cook in Radarange oven 15 to 20 minutes or until fruit is tender. Stir every 5 minutes. Strain juice, using several thicknesses of cheesecloth or jelly bag. Measure juice, return to oven. Bring to boil (about 10 minutes), add sugar, using ¾ to 1 cup sugar to each cup of juice. Stir well. Cook about 30 minutes, stirring at 5 minute intervals. With candy thermometer test temperature; should read 220° when removed.

Ladle into sterilized glasses. Paraffin at once. Adjust covers when cool, and attach labels. Fills 3 to 5 6-ounce jelly glasses, depending on quantity of juice produced.

Conventional Cooking:
1. *Combine fruits and water in kettle. Cook over moderate heat. As fruit cooks, mash down in kettle (use a wooden spoon). Strain through cheesecloth or jelly bag. Measure juice and return to kettle.*
2. *Bring juice to a boil, stir in 1 cup sugar to each cup juice. Cool until jelly "sheets" from spoon. Proceed as directed.*

MULLED WINE PUNCH

2 tablespoons each whole cloves, allspice berries, and broken stick cinnamon
4 cups boiling water
3 to 4 tablespoons instant tea
1 can (6 oz.) frozen tangerine or orange juice concentrate
2 cans (6 oz. each) frozen Hawaiian Punch concentrate
2 bottles rosé wine
Lemon slices

Tie spices loosely in a piece of cheesecloth, add to boiling water in a large deep bowl or casserole. Cook in Radarange oven 5 minutes. Remove spices, add tea and juice concentrates; cook in oven 5 minutes. Stir several times. Add wine. The wine should make the mixture just hot enough for drinking. If you wish it very hot, return to oven and cook 1 minute. Garnish with lemon slices. Makes about 3 quarts.

Conventional Cooking:
1. *Add spices as directed above to boiling water. Simmer for 5 minutes.*
2. *Remove spices and proceed as directed above, heating punch on medium heat about 20 minutes.*

PEACH CONSERVE

2 cups peaches, chopped
1 can (1 lb. 4 oz.) crushed
  pineapple, drained
6 peach pits

1 bottle (8 oz.) maraschino
  cherries, cut up, with the
  syrup
7½ cups sugar
1 bottle (6 oz.) liquid pectin

Combine first ingredients in 4-quart covered glass dish. Cover; cook in Radarange oven 10 minutes. Remove from oven, add sugar; stir well. Return to oven, uncovered, for 15 minutes; stir every 5 minutes. Mixture should be boiling. Stir in pectin. Return to oven, uncovered, for 10 to 15 minutes more. Temperature should read 220° when removed. Stir 5 minutes to cool. Remove pits. Ladle into sterilized jars or glasses; paraffin at once. Cover when cool. Attach labels. Fills approximately 10 6-ounce glasses.

Conventional Cooking:
1. Combine first 4 ingredients in large kettle. Cook over moderate heat, about 10 minutes, mashing down with wooden spoon as mixture cooks. Stir in sugar. Cook a minute or two; then add pectin and stir.
2. Bring to a boil. Cook rapidly for time indicated on bottle (usually 3 to 5 minutes). Proceed as directed.

Part III

DINING ABROAD AT HOME

During the last two decades Americans have become far less traditional in their eating patterns and far more interested in international cuisine.

As our servicemen returned from foreign countries and continents they brought with them an acquired taste for the foods served in these far-flung parts of the globe. Then Americans began to travel—more extensively than ever before—and they, too, brought back new ideas about food and cookery. As a result, family meals became more interesting and less monotonous.

With a Radarange microwave oven, both cooking and cleanup are easy and fast. So do try these recipes and menus in *your* home.

239

DINE ABROAD AT HOME

HAWAII

1.

Pork Chops *Maui**
Carrots and Bamboo Shoots — Buttered Rice*
Eggplant Salad
Coconut Ice Cream
Coffee

2.

Polynesian Medley*
Chinese Peas* — Raw Carrot Sticks
Pineapple Sherbet
Crème de Menthe
Coffee

ITALY

1.

Easy Lasagne*
Broccoli* with Slivered Almonds
Romaine Salad
Assortment of Fresh Fruit
Coffee

2.

Veal Scaloppine Milano*
Italian Eggplant* — Buttered Spaghetti*
Tossed Green Salad
Spumoni
Coffee

3.

Steak Palermo*
Buttered Zucchini* — Spaghetti with Tomato Sauce*
Italian Bread
Lemon Sherbet
Coffee

*Starred items are found in this cookbook.

FRANCE

1.

Chicken Breasts with Artichokes*
Petits Pois — Baked Potatoes*
Hot French Bread
Tossed Green Salad
Caramel Custard*
Demitasse

2.

Gourmet Beef Stew*
Hot Garlic Bread
Endive Salad
French Pastry
Demitasse

3.

Cornish Cassoulet*
Garden Lettuce and Orange Salad
Croissants
Rum Cake*
Demitasse

SPAIN

1.

Spanish Beef Roll*
Tomatoes and Mushrooms — Mashed Potatoes
Cucumber Salad
Caramel Custard*
Coffee

2.

Nachos*
Spanish Lamb Chops*
Green Pepper and Stuffed Olive Salad
Sherried Fruits
Coffee

*Starred items are found in this cookbook.

3.

Fish Costa Brava*
Tossed Green Salad
Hot Rolls
Orange Sherbet
Coffee

4.

Gazpacho
Braised Duckling Spanish Style*
Green Peas* — Mashed Potatoes
Raw Relishes
Melon Wedges
Coffee

RUSSIA

Garden Patch Borscht*
Beef Kabobs*
Best Green Beans* — Kasha
Celery — Olives
Spiced Fruit Compote*
Tea

GERMANY

1.

Hearty German Supper*
Pumpernickel
Celery — Radishes
Nut Torte with Whipped Cream
Coffee

2.

Sauerbraten*
Mashed Potatoes — Sweet-Sour Red Cabbage*
Celery — Olives
Apple Cake Dessert
Coffee

*Starred items are found in this cookbook.

3.

German Fresh Ham and Sauerkraut*
Potato and Carrot Kugel*
Green Salad
Baked Apples with Cream*
Coffee

1.

Chow Mein with Beef Heart*
Rice*
Preserved Kumquats
Almond Cookies
Tea

2.

Cantonese Ribs*
Bean Sprout Salad — Rice*
Pineapple Cubes
Rice Cookies
Tea

3.

Won Ton Soup
Chinese Rice and Crab*
Chinese Peas*
Ice Cream
Tea

SCOTLAND

Creamed Finnan Haddie*
Cabbage Sauté — Baked Potatoes*
Raw Vegetable Relishes
Spiced Fruit Compote*
Oatmeal Cookies
Tea

*Starred items are found in this cookbook.

1.

Dublin Lamb Stew*
Irish Soda Bread*
Watercress Salad
Peaches with Melba Sauce
Tea

2.

Cold Sliced Corned Beef
Colcannon*
Sliced Tomatoes and Onions
Fruited Cookie Squares*
Tea

MEXICO

Mexican Chicken*
Baked Wild and Long Grain Rice
Sliced Tomato Salad
Caramel Pumpkin Flan*
Coffee

REGIONAL AND HOLIDAY

NEW ENGLAND

Toll House Baked Beans*
Warm Brown Bread
Cole Slaw — Pickled Beets
Mocha Bread Custard*
Coffee

2.

New England Pot Roast*
Creamed Onions* — Baked Potatoes*
Hearts of Lettuce
Mystery Pudding Cake*
Coffee

*Starred items are found in this cookbook.

SOUTHERN

Texas Crab Casserole*
Carrot Circles — Buttered Okra*
Virginia Spoon Bread*
Southern Cream Cake*
Coffee

CALIFORNIA

Tangy Brown Ribs*
Barbecued Corn* — Vegetable Salad
Blueberry Muffins*
Citrus Stuffed Melon
Coffee

MIDWEST

Glazed Smoked Pork Butt*
Scalloped Corn* — Lemon Potatoes*
Hot Biscuits
Perfection Salad
Cherry Pie
Coffee

THANKSGIVING

Roast Turkey*
Buttered Onions and Walnuts* — Sherried Sweets*
Cranberry Sauce*
Celery — Olives — Pickles
Pumpkin Pie
Coffee

CHRISTMAS

Spiced Cider Baked Ham*
Creamy Green Beans and Mushrooms* — Baked Potatoes*
Orange Beets*
Jellied Cranberry Salad
Peppermint Ice Cream
Coffee

*Starred items are found in this cookbook.

INDEX

251